# A Living Witness

Dr. Dolores Floyd

Edited by Rev. Dr. Harriet S. Gainer

Cover design by Douglas Stout;
P.B. Studios (www.pbstudios.net)

Contact the author: alwdhf2010@gmail.com

*Amended 2020*

Beloved Publisher
P.O. Box 4562
Albany, GA 31706
https://www.belovedpublisher.com

# Dedication

I would like to thank God for being a witness to these testimonies and for making all of this possible. *I would like to dedicate this book to: my husband, John Floyd; my daughters, Tonescha LaShawn Sibley and Davina Jonette Floyd; my son, John Emmanuel Floyd Jr.; my mother-in-law, the late Dorothy Floyd; my father-in-law, the late Willie Lee Floyd; and my parents, Rev. Sammie L. Hart Sr. and the late Eva Bell Crawford Hart.*

# Endorsements

In this book, *A Living Witness*, Dolores Floyd takes the reader on her personal journeys as she and her family faces life battle after battle. What shall separate us from the love of God? Finances? Jobs? People? Many things come our way to distract and to discourage us, but Dr. Floyd becomes transparent enough for you to "view" the inner thoughts and responses of a true Christian while in the midst of difficult situations. Trials really come to take us out but trust and dependence on God is what makes us over-comers!

This book shows the believer since God is for us, it doesn't matter who or what will try to come against us. We win - period! When we exchange our spiritual, physical, and mental pains, hurts, insecurities and disappointments with God's strength, we at that very moment are *strong* and more than able to face and beat whatever comes our way.

Please allow *A Living Witness* to encourage your heart and to help you to know that God hears your prayers and that He will never leave you nor forsake you!

– Elder Orlando Thomas &
Evangelist Kimberly J. Thomas
Jacksonville, Florida

Through it all God kept you here and for a reason. Even through our trials and tribulations, God continues to keep us in his care. When some around you had given up on you and tried to get the dearest one (your husband) to give up – he and I kept the faith that through prayers we knew God was going to bring you through and back to us. Because of your humbleness and meekness God kept you here to show others that only if you believe, He will be with you in your darkest hour. I know that during my visiting you in the hospital – you stole away to talk with God. I am aware that you heard every word I said and every prayer that I prayed with you. You are a living example that God cares!

Brenda K. Whitaker

As a long time friend, brother in Christ and former pastor of Lois; it gives me great pleasure, pride, and inspiration to give a few comments concerning the writing of this book as a witness and goodness of God's presence in our lives. For many years of faith being tried, love being tested, and patience stretched to its limits, I have been moved and transformed with God's power and grace and the steadfast resilience I've seen built in Lois and her family.

My life has been richly blessed through the fellowship with the couple John & Lois and the children John Jr. & Davina as I watched God raise up the woman, the wife, and the mother.

God bless you as you launch out in the deep with this project.

Rev. Jim Ewing Sr.

"The delayed years were meant to be so that your book could have merit and worth."

Bishop Victor Powell

# Foreword

In life, we meet many people. Some of the people that we meet are good and some are not so good. As we go through life, we have many experiences and these experiences shape us into the person that we are. Some years ago, I was blessed and honored to meet the Floyd family and to become their pastor. Dr. Floyd is a woman of faith.

I read her book, and it is a spirit filled book. She talks about the morning of the accident and how excited she was to begin her career of teaching. Her life was altered by the accident but her faith was increased.

Reading her book will give hope to those that are going through anything. We are encouraged by the scripture:

> "Who shall separate us from the love of Christ: Shall tribulations, or distress, or persecutions, or famine, or nakedness, or peril, or sword?"
>
> Romans 8:35

Dr. Floyd has persevered through all of the changes in her life: being in a coma, loosing an unborn child, being in and loosing her possessions in a flood, being in a second car accident, loosing a mother and her brother, going through the pressures of graduate school while working as an educator, and staying committed through the highs and the lows of a marriage.

You will witness that her faith is uncompromised.

Dr. Floyd came from a coma to obtaining her Doctorate's degree. She is now on the minister's staff at New Beginning Missionary Baptist Church. I am so thankful to know Dr. Dolores Floyd. I look forward to reading many other books that she will write as well as listening to her preach God's Word.

May God bless you,
Pastor Solomon Loud Jr.
New Beginning Missionary Baptist Church
209 N. Monroe St.
Albany, GA 31721

# Foreword

This book is truly the witness of someone who has walked with God. If you are having difficulties finding your call in life, this book is a must read. The accounts of the author's life story in this book are inspiring and transformable for anyone who is attempting to find peace for their souls and joy for the times of confusion. This book is an in depth look at the soul of a child of God. Her experiences will bless those who don't know God as well as those who do.

The truths that you are about to receive, written by Dr. Dolores Floyd, are the same truths that I have been proclaiming for almost 16 years in the ministry and now at New Zion Hill M. B. Church. The truths are soul penetrating and will assure you of your destination in Jesus Christ. The book assures you that God has a purpose for all of our lives and it would behoove you to find your calling and stay with God. God is such an awesome God. He does what He wants, when He wants, and how He wants, because He is sovereign. The book will furthermore cast into your spirit-man an awesome awareness of purpose for your life.

For the Scripture teaches us in Romans 5:3-5 "And not only so, but we glory in tribulations also; knowing that tribulation worketh patience, and patience, experience; and experience, hope; and hope maketh not ashamed; because the love of God is shed abroad in our hearts by the Holy Ghost which is given unto us." You can rest assured that if you take the time to read it, this book will bless you and help to direct your path in Christ Jesus. Thanks be to God for Dr. Dolores Floyd for allowing the Holy Spirit to work through her.

Bishop O.D. Burton, Sr., Pastor
New Zion Hill M.B. Church
Albany, GA 31701

# Introduction

Have you ever been hurt, rejected, wounded, broken-hearted, devastated, depressed or worse? You will find that alcohol, drugs, sex, over-eating, or over spending only numbs the pain. I grew up with both of my parents, was raised in the church, and taught to forgive and to treat people the way that you want to be treated. Nevertheless, life can still bring changes that you can't predict. Bad or unfortunate things can happen to good people. As I look back over the first half of my life, I reflect and see that many events happened in my life that could have taken my joy, peace, and love or it could have left me broken and bitter.

Many people see the glory, in a person's life, but they just don't know the story. In this book, the Lord has allowed me to pull back the curtain on my life so that others can see the evidence of the power of God in action. I know that I am a survivor especially after experiencing two car accidents, sickness, a miscarriage, two floods, the highs and lows of marriage, the challenges of getting an advanced education, the loss of a classroom, a parent, both of my in-laws and a brother. Many nights I cried to the Lord and prayed for strength and direction.

The main focus of this book is my survival of an automobile accident that I had in 1990 which resulted in me being in a coma for two weeks. I could have died instantly or remained in a vegetative state. However, God reached down from heaven and spared my life so that I could be a living testimony. I clearly remember "a Voice with no face," beaming in front of me. A "Voice" gently called my name, "Dolores." To gain my total attention the "Voice" called my name again, "Dolores," and continued to say, "It's alright, don't be afraid. I'm not going to heal half of you; I'm going to heal all of you." Then the "Voice" left. At that point I had no idea what had happened to me or the seriousness of my accident. I am a living witness to my car accident and to other miracles which the Lord performed in my life over the course of nineteen years.

Isaiah 43:2 encourages us with these words, "When thou passest through the waters, I will be with thee; and through the rivers, they shall not overflow thee; When thou walkest through the fire, thou shall not be burned; neither shall the flame kindle upon thee." I thank God for his promises and for keeping everyone of them. I am a living witness that the Lord will protect you, hear you cry; save you, raise you up, and keep you together. He won't put more on you than you can bear. If that isn't enough, according to Psalms 138:8, the Lord will lead you, guide you, supply your needs, and He will teach you what you need to know. He will bring you out. Not by might, nor by power, but by my spirit saith the Lord. (Zechariah 4:6)

I have scars and I remember the events, but praise God, I don't feel the pain or hold any resentment. I believe that that the best part of my life is ahead of me. Moreover, Isaiah 61:7 states, "For your shame ye shall have double..." To me, that means that I shall have double for my trouble. My husband and I felt the strain and the suffering of me loosing my health, my first classroom, an unborn child, our home, and family members. Like the story of Job, I know that after our trials, the Lord blessed the latter end more than the beginning. Giving the glory to God and not to material things, my husband and I received more than what we had before our trials and tribulations. My health is restored, we have two beautiful children and a home to call our own. Now I am a Professional School Counselor and I teach a lesson in each classroom. I have also earned two Masters' degrees, a specialist and a doctorate degree.

I agree with the sentiments of Marvin Sapp, when he said, "I never would have made it without God. I know for a fact that I would have lost it all. But now I see how He was there for me. Now I can say that, I'm stronger; I'm wiser, I'm so much better."¹ My past developed me into the person that I am today. I know that the Lord has allowed me to go through a metamorphosis because I'm not naïve like I use to be. A lot of innocence and fear has been shredded from my character; my character has been refined. I know where I've been and I know what the Lord has brought me through. I am a living witness to the words of Romans 8:37, "Nay, in all these things we are more than conquerors through him that loved us." It is no secret what God can do, and what He has done for others, He'll do for you. Always remember that God can restore you. So, don't give up and don't quit. Every event in your life is for a season; it's temporary. I'm so glad that trouble don't last always and that joy cometh in the morning.

I believe that God allows us to experience the peaks and the valleys of life in order that we may be equipped to lead and encourage others (Arnette, 1997). ² I believe this is true as well as the statement made by Dr. K. A. Arnette, "I survived my past so that God can use me for his purpose (personal communication, September 10, 2005)." After reading this book, it is our family prayer that you will have the courage and the strength to go through everything that you have to face in your life. Psalms 18:28-29 tells us, "For thou will light my candle; the Lord my God will enlighten my darkness. For by thee I have run through a troop; and by my God have I leaped over a wall."

Now Lord, may all that You have created, birthed, and developed in me be used to bring hope and encouragement to others. It is our hope that this book will bring glory to Your Holy name. The time has come for me to share my testimony with those who are about to experience a miracle, going through trials and tribulations, or coming out of a miracle from God.

## Chapter One

*I will praise Thee, oh Lord with my whole heart;*
*I will shew forth all Thy marvelous work.*
*I will be glad and rejoice in Thee:*
*I will sing praise to Thy name,*
*O Thou Most High.*
Psalms 9:1-2 (KJV)

## This is The Day!

In 1989, two events occurred that seemed to make my life complete. The first event occurred on September 6. John and I had our first baby; after having tried unsuccessfully for four years. The second event occurred in November when I became a Fourth Grade Teacher. I loved teaching Fourth Grade. It was like a child having her wish come true after blowing out the candles on her birthday cake. This reminded me of the saying; "Good things come to those who wait." The Lord knows I've waited. And now, I'm going to make the best of every moment of this part of my life; the good, the bad, and the ugly parts.

## Two Months Later

The day was January 8, 1990. The day finally arrived! I had been dreading and anticipating this day at the same time. It was the day my *Teaching Professional Assessment Inventory (TPAI)* was due at the school where I had just been hired as a Fourth Grade Teacher. I had a lot of emotions flowing through me that morning. I know that I was exhausted from completing all the requirements for my portfolio, but I was also thankful to the Lord for my work because I felt that I had done a thorough job. As I reflected back, how much *I thanked God for the experience that He allowed me to go through as a lab technician at the Vocational Technical School's Child Care Department in Albany, Georgia. My supervisor was tough and I would get upset with her because she expected nothing less than quality work from me. Now I can see the importance of all she required.*

With all of these feelings dancing inside my mind, I happily got dressed for work. I placed my teaching materials, the baby bag, and my four-month-old baby boy in the car.I remember thinking, *I can't believe it! The things that I have been praying about for so long were beginning to happen.* While I was driving my four-month-old baby boy to my friend LaDedra's house, who agreed to watch our son as I started my new job, I can remember feeling so thankful to the Lord, so I started to sing. I thought about how the Lord had blessed my husband and me with this handsome baby boy. He was worth the wait. I continued singing with added joy.

*"This is the day; this is the day that the Lord has made.*

*That the Lord has made;*
*We will rejoice, we will rejoice and be glad in it; and*
*be glad in it.*
*This is the day that the Lord has made.*
*We will rejoice and be glad in it.*
*This is the day; this is the day that the Lord, has*
*made."*

It was a cool day outside but it didn't seem to matter because I was warmed by the feeling of satisfaction that you get when you finally complete a project. When I arrived at the baby-sitter's house, I hugged my son and gave him a goodbye kiss before I went to work. Unfortunately or should I say fortunately, that is all that I remember of that day, except for a few fuzzy details.

**The Voice and the promise**

I can remember being lifted, while my body was held straight, from what seemed like a hard or firm surface to another hard or firm surface, over different periods of time. I also remember being rolled down a long corridor. I'm not sure however, if all of this was during the same day. Nevertheless, I strongly remember "**A Voice** with no face, beaming in front of me." **The Voice** gently called my name, "Dolores, Dolores, It's alright, don't be afraid."

It is important for me to mention that I didn't have any idea of what had happened or what was happening to me. All I know is I didn't say anything. I couldn't see anything but darkness and the beam in front of me. I don't remember feeling anything but peace. Everything was so nice, calm, and peaceful. In spite of these feelings of serenity, my physical body must have been afraid, nervous, or responding in a jittery manner because **The Voice** told me not to be afraid. Immediately, peace came and I wasn't afraid anymore.

    **The Voice** continued and said, "I'm not going to heal half of you, I'm going to heal ALL of you," and then **The Voice** left.

### The Glory of the Lord

    According to Luke 2:9 (KJV), the Bible speaks of the Glory of the Lord after Mary wrapped her firstborn son in swaddling clothes and then laid Him in the manger. In the same country there were shepherds watching over their sheep. Moreover, the Bible states that when the angel of the Lord came to the shepherds, the Glory of the Lord shone around about them (Luke 2:9). And the angel said unto them, "Fear not, for, behold, I bring you good tiding of great joy, which shall be to all people. For unto you is born this day in the city of David a Savior, Which is Christ the Lord."

    In addition to this, the Glory of the Lord was also seen during the transfiguration of Christ. Before the transfiguration occurred, the Lord took Peter, James, and John to a high mountain. These men saw Jesus' appearance change in front of them and His face did shine as the sun, and His clothes were white as the light (Matthew 17:2; KJV). According to Matthew 17:4, it is also written that during this time, Moses and Elias appeared and talked with Jesus. Peter's reply was, "Lord, it is good for us to be here." While Peter was speaking, a bright cloud came over them. And a voice came out of the cloud and said,

*This is my beloved Son, in whom I am well please, hear ye Him. Matthew 17:5b (KJV)*

When the Lord shows us His power and Glory He does not want us to be afraid. In Genesis 15:1, "the Word of the Lord came to Abram in a vision, saying, Fear not, I am thy shield and thy exceeding great reward." The Lord promised to do a mighty work in Abram's life and knew that Abram would also need His shield of protection around him.

**The Accident**

Later, I learned sparingly from my husband John Floyd, that I had been involved in an automobile accident. The left front tire had blown out on my car shortly after I had dropped our baby off to the baby-sitter. The car I was driving, a 1988 Toyota, went over the median and crossed over two lanes where it was in the middle of on-coming traffic. A middle-aged woman driving a van ended up hitting me. Both of our vehicles ended up on the embankment of the Flint River Bridge, which is located on Oakridge Drive.

The newspaper article from the Albany Herald ("Two Hospitalized," 1990)[4] stated the driver of the Toyota was traveling east when she apparently slid sideways into the lane of westbound traffic causing a 1979 van to strike her with its left front fender.

According to the article, I was pinned inside my vehicle for at least 30 minutes while rescuers removed a door and a seat to reach me. The paramedics had to use the "Jaws of Life" to release me from the car. The spokesman who wrote the article said both drivers were 'incapacitated' and the identities of either driver was not available.

## The Good Samaritan

It is my belief that God will always take care of His people. When you can not speak for yourself or if you are in a situation that seems impossible; that is when God shows up and takes control of the situation. He specializes in things that are impossible to man.

*But Jesus beheld them and said unto them, "With men this is impossible; but with God all things are possible."* Matthew 19:26 (KJV)

Additionally, a similar Scripture found in Luke 1:37 (KJV), states "For with God nothing shall be impossible."

At that moment my co-worker Jocylin, who I will refer to as the good Samaritan, was on her way to take her seventeen month old baby girl to the baby sitter when she noticed a car crossing over on the other side of the traffic. *"Why is that car coming over here?"* she asked herself. There were a couple of cars in front of her, but she could tell that something was not right. All of a sudden, she witnessed a van hit my car. My car spun around and was half way across the street. A Caucasian man, who I will refer to as the Unsung Hero, pulled over and so did the Good Samaritan to see if the passengers were okay and how they could help. I was told much later that because of the swelling and bleeding on my face, my co-worker didn't even realize that it was me.

Her eyes quickly scanned the car and she noticed a baby car-seat. After looking around with no success, she nervously said, "Oh no! Where is the baby?"

The unsung hero said, "I need you to go and call for help and I'll stay and direct traffic."

The Good Samaritan felt her knees and body shaking, but managed to go to a pay phone that was nearby and called 911. Cell phones were not popular at that time.

"There has been an accident on Oakridge Drive", a voice interrupted saying, "Someone has already called and the police and ambulance are on their way."

Not being in any shape to drive, the Good Samaritan called her husband, who came and took their baby to the baby-sitter and then took her to work. When my co-worker finally arrived at school, she explained to the office personnel why she was late and that others would probably be late because of an automobile accident that delayed traffic on Oakridge Drive. An hour later, the Principal went to the Good Samaritan's room and told her he had been informed that it was I who had been in the accident. She fell apart again but said she wanted to remain at work. The Good Samaritan and I were newly hired teachers so both of us were going through the Teacher Professional Assessment Inventory (TPAI); therefore, we shared a bond. After work, she went to the hospital to check on my condition and to talk with my husband. I was still in bad shape and had gone into a coma.

# Guiding Principles/Supportive Scriptures

- This is the day that the Lord has made, we will rejoice and be glad in it. Psalm 118:24 (KJV)

- Live each day as if it is your last and your last day as if you'll live forever. (Author unknown)

- What is not always what it appears to be. Only God can turn a bad situation around and use it for His good. For example, Joseph said, "But as for you, ye thought evil against me, but God meant it unto good, to bring to pass, as it is this day, to save much people alive." Genesis 50:20 (KJV)

- I came to know God as Jehovah Rohi (Je-ho-vah Roha)- God is our Shepherd.[5] Surely, the Lord Jehovah-Rohi, my Shepard, reached His staff down from Heaven and cushioned the impact of the van. Yes, it could have been worse. When that wasn't enough, He stood in front of me and spoke a promise in my ear; which I shall never forget.

- God is not a man that He should lie; neither is He the Son of man that He should repent: hath He saith, and shall He not do it, or has He spoken, and shall He not make it good. Numbers 23:19 (KJV)

**Let us pray:**

Father, in the Mighty name of Jesus I pray that You forgive me for my sins. I thank You for Your Mighty hand that reached down from Heaven, and spared my life. **Thank You for allowing me to be a "Living Witness" from my accident** in such a way that the memory from it would not hurt me, but bring Glory to your name. Now Lord, I pray for people everywhere. Protect their going out and their coming in. May you continue to be the good shepherd and protect us from dangers seen and unseen. In Jesus' Mighty name I pray, amen.

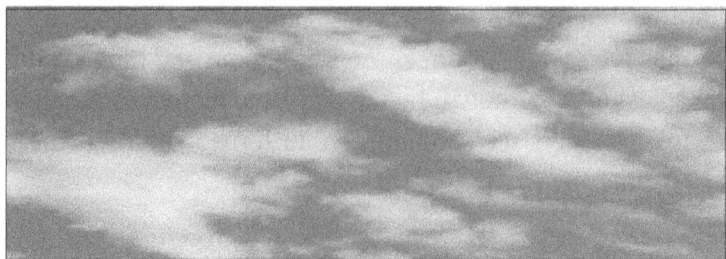

## Chapter Two

*And Jesus answering saith unto them, Have faith in God.*
*For verily I say unto you, that whosoever shall say unto*
*this mountain, Be thou removed an be thou cast unto the*
*sea; and shall not doubt in his heart, but shall believe that*
*those things which he saith shall come to pass; he shall*
*have whatsoever he saith.*
*Mark 11:23 (KJV)*

# The Prayer of Faith

It was not long after my husband arrived at work that he
received a telephone call from my Principal at the elementary school where I was worked, informing him that I had
been involved in a car accident. John said he can remember
thinking, he didn't say anything about the baby so I guess
he is alright. John was afraid to ask this question, so he kept
thinking; I got to get to the hospital. I got to get to the hospital. One of John's co-workers saw that he wasn't in any
shape to drive so he drove him to the hospital.

The Security Officer dropped John off to the hospital and
drove off as he knew that John needed to be alone with his wife.
While this was an admirable act of friendship and workman-

ship, it still left John without a means of transportation because, I wasn't a patient at the hospital where he was dropped off. Without giving it much thought, John just took off running to the next hospital, which was approximately two miles away. John, joking about this serious moment said, "As I think back, if someone had stopped and asked me if I needed a ride, I probably would have said 'No thank-you. I'm kind of in a hurry.'"

When John arrived at the hospital where I was admitted, he had to wait because the doctors were working on me. As John stood and looked, he could see the clothes that I had on before I left for work discarded on a cart. He knew that they belonged to me because he ironed my clothes the night before. When he looked at my clothes again, he noticed that they had been cut so that they could be taken off me. He knew then that I must have gotten hurt pretty badly.

**The Report**

According to the History and Physical Examination Report, and the X-Rays, I was unconscious and was unresponsive to anything but deep pain stimuli but did move extremities; my right arm only moved slightly toward my body. I had a closed head injury with cerebral contusion. An obvious contusion, swelling, and a small laceration were present on the right side of my face. There was a considerable amount of swelling over the right side of the face and cheek which extended somewhat into the scalp. I also had lacerations on the left leg and right arm with some skin loss. A punctured wound to the left inner ankle was noted. X-rays indicated a fracture of the first two ribs on the right and one on the left. [6] In every day terms, I had several broken ribs, and my right cheekbone was also broken.

I was admitted to Surgical Intensive Care Unit (SICU) from the Emergency Room (ER) via stretcher. Nursing progress notes indicated that I was comatose. Appropriate care and dressings were applied to my other injures during this period. My husband was called back to SICU to encourage me to talk. I did not respond to his voice; only to painful stimuli. When I was restless I would kick the covers off with my left leg, and when I became very restless my left wrist had to be restrained with light restraint to keep me from pulling IV lines. Even though my eyes were closed and I did not talk, I was able to squeeze a hand with my left hand when asked. Both of my legs would move about in the bed, but I could not bend the right leg. [7]

An incision was made under my right eye to repair my cheekbone. The fractured area had to be cleaned since the fracture was more than two weeks old. A #26 gauge wire was used in the frontal area and a 28 gauge wire was used inferiorly in a figure eight form. The fracture was realigned, and the defect became less noticeable.I have two cuts, approximately one inch wide and two inches long on my left leg. The doctors could not close up my cuts with stitches because I had been in a coma for two weeks. Moreover, the deep wide gash or cut under my right arm near my elbow also did not get stitched. I could not extend or raise my right arm very high. Neither could I turn my neck to the right or to the left side very far. In addition to this, I could not walk on my right leg.

I was told that the driver of the other vehicle also had some injuries and was hospitalized in the same hospital. I'm sorry that I did not know the full extent of her injuries nor could do anything about them.   But I'm glad that the Lord took care of her as well me.

## The Power of Prayer

I am told that word of my accident traveled fast and that people from all over heard and prayed for my recovery. Prayers were being prayed for me in the North, South, East, and on the West Coast. James 5:16 (KJV) states, "The effectual fervent prayer of a righteous man availeth much."

Family and friends tried to visit me but my husband said the doctors stated that only immediate family would be allowed to see me until I came out of the coma. I can imagine that had to be an awfully hard job for John to enforce because the family probably put a lot of pressure on him when they wanted to see their loved one. Nevertheless, John stood firm, regardless of who didn't like it; he followed the doctor's orders because he felt the doctor's knew what was best for me. The doctors felt that it would not be a good idea for me when I came out of the coma and saw a lot of people, family or strangers, just looking at me. All the excitement could be too overwhelming and could cause me to slip back into the coma.

I'm glad that the Lord knows what is best for us, even when we don't know. The Lord will send His angels to watch over and to protect us. The Bible tells me so:

*The angel of the Lord encampeth around about them that fear Him.* Psalms 34:7 (KJV)

*In their entire affliction he was afflicted, and the angel of His presence saved them; and He bared them and carried them all the days of old.*
Isaiah 63:9 (KJV)

I know the Lord put it in John's spirit to obey the doctors, and to watch over me. I thank the Lord for giving my husband the strength to say "No" to family and friends.

While I was in a coma, my husband said that the hospital staff talked to him about the possibility of me being in a vegetative state even if I came out of the coma. It was also mentioned that he would need someone to help take care of the baby and I.

In despair and helplessness John cried out to the God, "Why me Lord?"

John said that the response came back in his spirit, "Who would you wish this on?"

John thought, *no one* Lord, and he later confessed that if anyone could make it through these injuries, it was I. Praise God for that faith!

**I am a living witness that prayer changes things.** I think about the Scriptures that says,

*"Is any sick among you? Let him call for the elders of the church; and let them pray over him, anointed him with oil in the name of the Lord.*

*And the prayer of faith shall save the sick, and the Lord shall raise him up; and if he has committed sins, they shall be forgiven him, Confess your faults one to another, and pray one for another, that ye may be heal."*
James 5:16 (KJV)

### What Do You Do While You Wait on God?

During this time, I was a member of a Holiness church. My cousin Gwen and sister-in-the-Lord, now a minister, had a fervent spirit and was a prayer warrior. She supervised the ladies at the church to sing and pray for me around the clock. Another sister in the Lord said they specifically prayed that I would live and be reserved, and that God would restore my life. I am told that my aunt Pricilla, a strong woman of God, prayed and sang constantly around the family at the hospital. **I am a living witness that there is deliverance in the combination of prayer and singing.** The Scriptural bases for this can be found in Acts 12:5-7 (KJV).

*When Peter was in prison, the Scripture states how the church prayed unto God, without ceasing, for his deliverance. Peter was sleeping; bound with chains and guarded by two soldiers on either side and a soldier in front of the prison door, when a bright light appeared and the angel of the Lord stood before Peter. When the angel said, "Get dress," the chains fell off Peter. At first Peter thought it was a vision; then he realized it was the Lord God.*

Another female minister, Rev. Dr. Harriett Gainer who has her doctorate in Ministry and whom I considered my mother in the Lord, insisted that healing tapes of someone sharing passages from the Bible be constantly played in my room. She knew that there was research that cautioned family members who were around someone in a coma to be mindful of what they said or discussed around them. The patient is able to hear what is being said; even though they may not be able to respond. The Reverend Doctor Gainer also knew the power of the spoken words from the Holy Bible.

She said, "If Dolores can hear anything, I want her to hear the Word on healing."

So, she brought a tape recorder and tapes with healing Scriptures to the hospital and asked the nurses to play the tapes on healing. Thank God for the saints of **God** calling for the elders in the church and for that persistent attitude!

A Biblical example for this can be found in Luke 7:1-9 (KJV). A Centurion had a servant, who was dear to him, that was sick unto death. When the Centurion heard about Jesus, he sent the elders of the Jews to ask Him to come and heal his servant. The Centurion didn't feel worthy to go to Jesus himself or for Him to come under the roof of his house. Nevertheless, the Centurion had the faith that if Jesus just sent the Word, his servant would be healed. Jesus marveled at the Centurion's great faith and said, "I have not found so great faith, no, not in Israel." When the elders of the Jews returned home, they found the Centurion's servant completely healed (Luke 7:10).

Additionally, I'm reminded of the two cases that caused two individuals to press through the crowd of people that came to see Jesus for their healing. One case involved a man by the name of Jairus; ruler of the synagogue, who had a daughter that was dying. The other case involved a woman "having an issue of blood" for twelve yearsShe had spent all her money upon physicians that couldn't help her. Both cases needed a healing from Jesus at the same time.

Jairus fell at Jesus' feet and besought Him to come into his house to heal his only daughter who was twelve years old. At the same time, the woman "having the issue of blood" believed that if she could just touch the hem of His garment, she could be made whole. The woman came behind Jesus and touched the border of His garment. Immediately she was made whole.

Jesus responded and said, "Who touched me?"

The woman came trembling and fell down before Him and gave the testimony of what had happened to her.

## Is anything too hard for God?

According to the Scripture found in Luke 8:48 (KJV), Jesus said, "Daughter, be of good comfort, thy faith has made thee whole; go in peace."

At that same moment, a ruler of the synagogue came and gave the report, "Thy daughter is dead, trouble not the Master."

When Jesus heard this He said, "Fear not: believe only, and she shall be made whole."

Jesus went to Jairus' house, He only allowed Peter, James, John, and the parents of the child to go in. Jesus told them not to cry and gave the report that the girl was not dead, she was just asleep. Jesus ended up putting everyone out because they laughed at Him, knowing that she was already dead.

Operating in faith, Jesus took the daughter by the hand and said, "Maid, arise." Her spirit came again, and she got up. He commanded them to give her something to eat. Her parents were astonished. Luke 8:55-56 (KJV)

Moreover, when I later read information on the topic of being in a comatose state, the information I found confirmed what the Reverend Doctor Gainer believed. According to the research from The Mayo Foundation for medical education and research (May 17, 2006) [8], if someone visits a family member who is in a coma, they should talk to him or her in their regular tone of voice. If having a conversation with others nearby, you are to assume that a comatose patient can hear you and understand what you're saying. Even though he or she may not respond to stimuli and appears to lack consciousness, some people who have emerged from a coma have reported remembering others' conversations.

## Guiding Principles/Supportive Scriptures

- For we are saved by hope: but hope that is seen is not hope: for what a man seeth, why does he yet hope for? But if we hope for that we see not, then do we with patience wait for it. Romans 8: 24-25 (KJV)

- I came to know God as Jehovah-Shalom; the Lord is Peace.[9]

- Faith is the substance of things hoped for, the evidence of things not seen. Hebrew 11:1 (KJV)

- If thou shall say unto this mountain be thou removed and cast unto the sea; it shall be done. Mark 11:23 (KJV)

- We walk by faith and not by sight. 2 Corinthians 5:7 (KJV)

- Jesus said unto him, "If thou canst believe all things are possible to him that believeth." Mark 9:23 (KJV)

- Without faith, it is impossible to please Him: for he that cometh to God must believe that He is and that He is a rewarder of them that diligently seek Him. Hebrew 11:6 (KJV)

- Even so faith, if it hath not works, is dead, being alone. James 2:17 (KJV)

- Paul wrote in I Corinthian 2:1 (KJV), That your faith should not stand in the wisdom of men, but on the power of God.

**Let us pray**

Father, in the name of Jesus, I pray that You forgive me for my sins. I want to thank You for hearing the prayers of Your saints and for healing my body. In the Mighty name of Jesus, and through the power of the Holy Spirit, I pray that patients will believe Your report and that their faith will rest in the power of God, and not only in men; especially when doctors have given up on them. In Jesus' Mighty name I pray, amen.

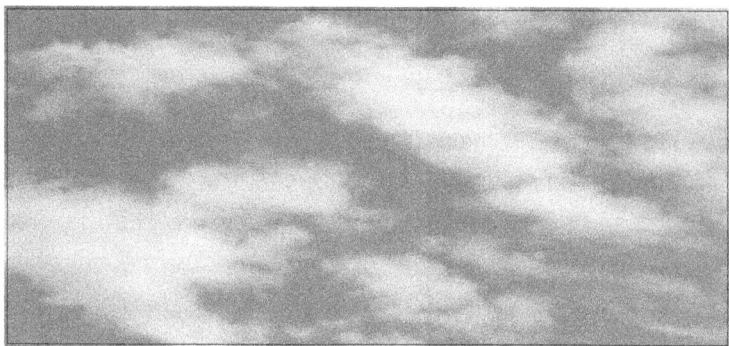

## Chapter Three

*... beareth all things, believeth all things,*
*hopeth all things, endureth all things.*
I Corinthians 13:7 (KJV)

# Love Lifted Me

My sister-in-law Gloria, kept John Jr. "(little man)" most of the time while John Sr. visited me at the hospital. She remembers that there were so many people, coming in and out of the hospital, who wanted to see me (personal communication, May 15, 2006). They just want to see my face and touch me. This would give them hope in feeling that I would be alright. She said, "Every day you could hear everyone in the waiting room saying, 'Did she wake up yet? Or, is she awake yet?'" This was the talk in the hospital everyday. Everyone asked this same question everyday until I *Woke Up!*

## I'm Awake Now

My husband said that when I came out of the coma, the first thing that I asked him was "Where were you while I was away talking with God?" I don't actually remember the conversation that I had with the Lord.

However, *I remember being left with a very strong impression that God truly wants to bless us, as believers, and that He has so much to give us. He can't or He won't because too many of us are jealous of each other, or talk about each other behind the other person's back. We are hindering our own blessings.*

I believe my family was just glad that I came out of the coma and didn't take what I said seriously. In fact, no one even mentioned what I said anymore; but I remember.

After the doctors checked and monitored my progress, they thought it would be a great idea to bring the baby in the hospital room to see me.

Instead of being happy to see the baby, John said that I just looked at the baby and then looked at him and said, "Would someone please get this crying baby."

Although this was not the response that the doctors hoped for, it was a normal reaction. I was now allowed to have visitors come to the hospital and visit with me.

**Visitation**

I don't want to hurt anyone's feelings, especially not the Hart family (my family) or the Floyd family (John's family), but of all the people who I'm told came to the hospital to visit me, I can only remember one visitor. This lady's name is Brenda. She was the secretary of the school, where I was a paraprofessional for three years. She was also a member of a Baptist Church, where I joined when I first moved to Albany in 1983.

I'm not sure why she made such a strong impression on my mind. It seem like she was there every day. Every time I opened my eyes, Brenda was looking at me like I was her daughter or a very close friend.

I remember constantly pleading with her, "Brenda, please go home and see about your family. "I'm okay." Brenda would just quietly and persistently say, "Don't worry; everything is going to be alright."

It felt like I literally had an angel watching over me. That was alright because I knew I could go to sleep and everything would be okay. I could let go; the Lord had everything under control. Reflecting on that time in my life reminds me of the song, "I've Got Angels Watching Over Me"[10]. I could hear the chorus of the song in my ears:

*I've got angels watching over me (Watching my way both night and day).*
*I've got angels watching over me (Fanning away the hurt, the pain).*
*I've got angels watching over me (They'll never fly away}.*
*Angels over me.*

I thank God for my angels, however, my husband said sleep was the last thing that I wanted to do. I would reply, "I've already slept too much." There was a sense of urgency to get up and do whatever God wanted me to do. It was important to work when I could and while I could do it. Each day was important, because I learned that tomorrow isn't promised to any one.

*Ecclesiastes 9:10 (KJV) says, Whatsoever thy hand findeth to do, do it with thy might; for there is not work, nor devise, nor knowledge, nor wisdom, in the grave, whither thou goest.*

My hospital stay lasted for about a month. I am a living witness that prayer is real and that it works. There are many people who offered some type of help that was significant during this dark period in my life. Please forgive me if I did not acknowledge the help that you my have contributed-no matter how large or small-**God** will recompense and reward you accordingly. I truly appreciate everyone's help, love, and prayers. Therefore; I want to reflect on a song that I love so much to expresses my appreciation:

> Love lifted me, Love lifted me,
> When nothing else would work,
> Love lifted me.
> Love lifted me, Love lifted me,
> When nothing else would work,
> Love lifted me.

## Guiding Principles/Supportive Scriptures

- Love lifted me, love lifted me. When nothing else would help, love lifted me.

- I came to know God as Jehovah- Elyon; the Lord God Most High.[11] I have Victory.

- But without faith it is impossible to please Him: for he that cometh to God must believe that He is and that He is a rewarder of them that diligently seek Him. Hebrew 11: 6 (KJV)

- But, beloved, be not ignorant of this one thing, that one day is with the Lord as a thousand years, and a thousand years as one day...the Lord is not slack concerning His promise as some men count slackness; but is long suffering to us-ward, not willing that any should perish, but that all should come to repentance. II Peter 3:8-9 (KJV)

- Because thou hast made the Lord, which is my refuge, even the Most High, thy habitation: there shall no evil befall thee, neither shall any plague come nigh thy dwelling. For He shall give His angels charge over thee, to keep thee in all thy ways. They shall bear thee up in their hands, lest thou dash thy foot against a stone. Psalms 91:9-12 (KJV)

- He that receiveth a prophet in the name of a prophet shall receive a prophet's reward; and he that receiveth a righteous man in the name of a righteous man shall receive a righteous man's reward. Mathew 10:41(KJV)

- …Weeping may endure for a night, but joy cometh in the morning. Psalms 30:5 (KJV)

- Behold, the eye of the Lord is upon them that fear Him, upon them that hope in His mercy; to deliver their soul from death, and to keep them alive in famine. Psalms 33: 18-19 (KJV)

- A new commandment I give unto you. That ye love one another as I have loved you, that ye also love one another. By this shall all men know that ye are My disciples; if ye have love one to anotherJohn 13:34-35 (KJV)

**Let Us Pray**
Father, in the Mighty name of Jesus, I pray that You forgive me for my sins and short comings. I thank You for Your love and for Your omnipresence. Thank You for keeping me as You healed my traumatized body and for waking me up out of my coma. Lord, I want to thank You for the angels that kept me safe. Help us to love one another as You love us, in Jesus' Mighty name I pray, amen.

## Chapter Four

*That ye be not slothful, but followers of them who through faith, and patience inherit the promises.*
Hebrew 6:12 (KJV)

# Faith and the Promise

While I was in the hospital, a nurse had to bathe me daily for a month and after I came home from the hospital, my husband bathed and dressed me daily for almost two months. As I mentioned earlier, I could not walk on my right leg; therefore, I had to use a walker when I got home from the hospital to get around.

## A Mother's Love

People from all over continued to call and pray for me to recover. My mother (the late Eva Bell Hart) came down from Pennsylvania and stayed with us for three months while I recuperated. I slept on and off most of the time. My mother cooked, cleaned, and took care of the baby too.

Thank God for mothers who give and sacrifice for their children, no matter how young or old they may be, on a continuous basis. I was still not allowed to pick up the baby because my ribs were still healing on their own. Sometimes when my mother would cook or clean up the house, she would put John Jr. in his car-seat and sit him on the bed beside me. I would play with him by touching his face or by stroking his hair. Sometimes, I would just give him his bottle.

As John sucked on his bottle, I would look at him and think *he is so handsome, Lord thank You for blessing us with this handsome baby boy*.

Then I softly said, *"Little Man, It took four years for you to get here, and I know* God *didn't bring us this far to leave us. Hang in there and with the help of the Lord, mama is going to get better. "*

I remember when I used to get terribly criticized by women because I didn't have a baby. Women who were usual church-goers and the women who seldom attended church would make comments such as: "She can afford to buy that because she doesn't have any children" or "She can afford to go to such a place because she doesn't have any children." I never realized how mean and insensitive some women could be towards another woman who didn't have any children. They just didn't know how much I wanted, hoped for, and prayed to have a baby or how many home pregnancy tests I had tried, only to be disappointed time after time.

The comments and the disappointments really hurt badly. It felt like someone had picked up stones and was taking turns piercing my heart. I didn't say anything; like Hannah, I just prayed unto the Lord. One evening after prayer meeting was over, my cousin Gwen and sister-in-the

Lord came over to me and said that the Lord showed her that I was going to conceive and bare a child. I was thrilled! I took God at His word. I knew that I had not shared my desire and prayers to the Lord with anyone.

Immediately I shared the news with my mother-in-law, Dorothy Floyd (now deceased). "Mom, God said that I am going to have a baby!" She smiled and said, "That's nice" being careful not to discourage me because she also believed in the power of God and wanted to share in my excitement. About a month later, it was confirmed by a medical doctor that I was going to have a baby! Praise God! On September 6, 1989, I conceived and had a son. We named him John Emmanuel (God is with us) Floyd.

"For this child I prayed; and the Lord has given me the petitions which I asked of Him."
I Samuel 1:27 (KJV)

I kissed our "Little Man" and softly said *"Lord, help me get better so that I can take care of the son that You blessed my husband and I with. I know You spared his life for a reason."* I wanted to pick my baby up so badly, but I knew I wasn't strong enough yet. So I waited. Nevertheless, each day, I could feel that I was getting stronger and stronger. I thank God for my step-daughter, Tonescha LaShaun Sibley, who was seven at the time and who has always been like a natural daughter to me. Sometimes she would help me watch "Little Man" when John would pick her up and bring her over to our house. Tonescha is so beautiful and sweet. She looks just like her daddy and walks like her grandmother, Dorothy Floyd. *Lord, help me to never mistreat her intentionally or unintentionally.*

**I Need You**

Even though I had the support of my mother and husband, I was afraid of being left alone. When you experience a near death experience, I believe it brings about feelings such as fear, doubt, dependency, and low self-esteem. Before the car accident I was a very confident and an independent wife. Now, I didn't want my husband out of my sight for very long; I clung to him constantly. I could feel that I was draining him, but I couldn't let go. I was even afraid of praying out loud. I felt that Satan would hear my prayers and try to stop them, delay my requests, or try to hurt me. I had forgotten that Satan's job was to kill (your dreams and hope), steal (what belongs to you) or to destroy (your character, hopes, or dreams). Needless-to-say, I couldn't or didn't think about God's plan to give us life and to give it more abundantly.

**The Promise**

I use to keep the television on the TBN (Trinity Broadcasting Network) gospel station. It seems a little funny to me now, but I didn't even realize that I wore glasses until I was stronger and wanted to watch television at home. I guess this wasn't very important to me when I was in the hospital. The Lord reminded me of the promise that He had made to me while I was in the hospital. The words came back to my remembrance:

**"Dolores, Dolores; don't be afraid. I'm not going to heal half of you. I'm going to heal all of you."**

I thought, *Wow! It was still hard to believe what had happened to me!* Immediately, I started lifting the promise that God made to me, back to Him in prayer. The scriptures say:

...So shall my word be that goeth forth out of my mouth: it shall not return unto me void, but it shall accomplish that which I please, and it shall prosper in the things whereto I sent it. Isaiah 55:11 (KJV)

And whatsoever ye shall ask in my name, that will I do, that the Father might be glorified through the Son. If ye shall ask anything in my name, I will do it.
John 14:13-14 (KJV)

And **Jesus** said unto the Centurion, Go thy way; and as thou hast believeth, so be it unto you. And his servant was healed the selfsame hour. Matthew 8:13 (KJV)


**A Prayer Warrior**

I had forgotten that I was a prayer warrior, and all the Scriptures that I had learned came flooding back to my mind. I began praying day and night and praising **God** constantly.

That reminded me of a praise song:

*The Lord inhabits the praises of His people.*
*So let's just praise Him, Let just praise Him.*
*The Lord inhabits the praises of His p-eo-ple.*
*So let's just praise the Lord. So let's just praise the Lord.*

I was no longer afraid of being left alone because you see, I was never alone. God was always with me. God's

Word said that He would never leave me; nor forsaken me. He would be with me always, even until the end. I believe God's Word to be true. **I'm a living witness that God will keep His promises.**

## Guiding Principles/Scriptures

- And if we know that He hears us, whatsoever we ask we know that we have the petitions that we desired of Him. I John 5:15 (KJV)

- I've come to know God as Jehovah-Nissi; The Lord is Conqueror.[12] The sign of conquest.

- The Lord has not given us the spirit of fear, but power, love, and a sound mind. II Timothy 1:7

- Let your conversation be without covetousness; and be content with such things as ye have for He hath said, I will never leave thee, nor forsaken thee. Hebrew 13:5 (KJV)

- For I will restore health unto thee, and I will heal thee of thy wounds, said the Lord; because they called thee an outcast, saying, this is Zion, whom no man seeketh after. Jeremiah 31:3 (KJV)

- We then that are strong ought to bear the infirmities of the weak, and not to please ourselves. Romans 15:1 (KJV)

- And He said unto me, My grace is sufficient for thee; for My strength is made perfect in weakness… Therefore I take pleasure in infirmities, in reproaches, in necessities, in persecutions, in distress for Christ's sake: for when I am weak, then am I strong. II Corinthians 12:9-10 (KJV)

**Let Us Pray:**

Father, in the name of Jesus, I pray that You will forgive me for my sins and short comings. I thank You that Your eyes are upon the righteous and Your ears are open to our cry. Thank You for giving us the petitions of our hearLord, thank You for the spirit of help that causes men and women, boys and girls to help another person when they are down or sick and can't help themselves. Help us to always trust in Your Word. In Jesus' Mighty name I pray, amen.

## Chapter Five

*He staggered not at the promises of God through unbelief,
but was strong in faith, giving glory to God; and being
fully persuaded, that what He had promised,
He was able also to perform.*
Romans 4:20-21(KJV)

# Restoration

My husband and I learned later of the significance of the
**voice**, which I believe was from **God**, calling me by my first
name the day of the car accident. If the Lord had said, "Get
up!" or "Rise!" everyone in the hospital or in the intensive
care unit would have gotten up. This is an awesome
thought!

**He Knows Your Name**

I recall two examples of this in the Bible where Jesus told a
person who was in an unconscious state to arise. One example can be found in John 11, when Lazarus, the brother of
Mary and Martha died.[13] When Lazarus was sick, the sisters
sent word to inform Jesus that Lazarus was sick.

They believed that Jesus would come and make him well, especially since Jesus was their friend and loved them. Jesus' response was contrary to what they anticipated.

"This sickness is not unto death but for the glory of God, that the Son of God might be glorified thereby." John 11:4 (KJV)

Jesus purposely waited two days before deciding to check on Lazarus. When Martha heard that Jesus was coming, she met Him and said, "Lord, if You had been here, my brother would not have died. But I know even now, whatsoever You ask of God, God will give it."

Lazarus had been in the grave for four days. Jesus said, "Thy brother shall rise again."
Mary fell to Jesus' feet and made the same comment her sister made to Jesus as she wept. Here we are allowed to see a glimpse of the humanity and the compassion of Jesus as He wept after He asked Mary where Lazarus was laid.

Jesus spoke with power to the grave as He said the words, "Said I not unto thee, that, if thou wouldest believe, thou shouldest see the glory of God."
After thanking God for hearing His prayers, He shouted with a loud voice "Lazarus, come forth." and Lazarus came forth (John 11:40, 43; KJV).

The second example occurred when Jesus, along with His disciples, went into a city called Nain. As He approached the gate of the city, a widow had a son who died and was being carried out. Jesus saw the woman and had compassion on her as He said, "Weep not."

Jesus touched the brier and they stopped. Then He proceeded to say, "Young man, I say unto thee, arise." The son who had died sat up and began to speak. Luke 7:11-15 (KJV)

**I Shall Rise and Walk**

Did I mention earlier that I had a walker? I was so embarrassed to use it. I would sit in the living room or kitchen and wait until any company would leave before I would get up and use it. I associated walkers with very old people and I was only thirty-one years old. Forgive me, Lord, for being foolish, selfish, and vain. I still didn't realize the extent and the seriousness of the accident. I used to stand at the side door in the kitchen and dream of walking to the mailbox to get the mail without using my walker. This goal inspired me and sent a wave of determination through my body to begin walking around the house without using the walker. I can remember standing up and holding onto the walls as I moved around to the different rooms in the house. I would hold onto the furniture in the room to reach an item that was in the middle of the room.

When I finally felt stronger, physically and spiritually I worked up the courage to walk from the kitchen door to the mailbox outside in the front yard. My cheek, on the right side of my face felt like Jell-O that was not quite jelled yet. I'm not sure how long it took me to walk to the mailbox. Needless to say, I felt like I was moving in slow motion but it didn't matter because, I did it! I did it all by myself. I walked to the mailbox and back to the house without using the walker. Hallelujah!!!

## Oh Happy Day

My last major prayer was to go to church on Easter Sunday for the first time since the accident without using a walker. My prayer was answered in April of 1990. Two sisters from the church (Pearl now a Pastor and Mary now an Evangelist) picked me up from my house and drove me to church.

Pearl, in reflecting back on that miracle, said, "I remember your short term memory was shot. When you talked, you asked the same questions over and over again." She continued talking and added, "You were mentally cloudy for a while. It took awhile for Dolores to emerge from behind a cloudy fog or wall. We could hear your voice, but it still wasn't you. "God shielded your mind from harm of any sort." (Personal Communication, November 10, 2007).

When we reached the church, they opened the door and helped me out of the car. Pearl recalled that I was still unsteady. Nevertheless, with grave determination and thanksgiving I walked in church that Easter Sunday for service without using the walker.

Everyone was surprised to see me and started praising God. You could hear moaning and groaning while others shouted "hallelujah!" and "Thank You Jesus!"

They saw the manifestation that their prayers had been answered and praised God for my healing. Tears of joy flooded my face along with cries of thanksgiving. **Oh, that was a happy day** that led to other happy days.

This victory gave me the courage to try driving again. The biggest challenge that I had was when I had to back out of the driveway and whenever I needed to use my right side mirror. Because of my injuries, I could only turn my neck slightly to the right. I would slowly practice going to the end of the street we lived on and then I would drive back to the house. I believe I practiced this for about three to four weeks and then I got the courage to drive around the block. This was as far as I would go without my husband. I never did have physical therapy, so my husband was very protective of everything that I did. Later, I shared this victory with my husband. He was glad for me, but he wasn't happy that I did any of this without him being present and there to help me.

**Mirror Mirror on the Wall**

Even though God gave me the strength to be victorious in accomplishing my goals of walking to the mailbox and with driving again, I had difficulty looking at myself in the mirror. In fact, I don't remember looking in the mirror very often as most ladies like to do because I felt that I looked so unattractive. My head was swollen and I looked physically different. As I mentioned earlier, an incision was made under my eye to repair my cheekbone. The right side of my face was very dry, rough, cracked, and disfigured. This was supposed to be good news because it was a sign that I was healing normally. Nevertheless, I felt apologetic that my husband and others had to look at me. I developed poor eye contact and my self-esteem decreased drastically. I deliberately selected clothing that were dark in color and garments that would not bring any special attention my way.

I remember that when I went back to the doctor's office for a check-up, the neurological surgeon and the plastic surgeon were both pleased with my recovery. In fact, the plastic surgeon expressed how drastically my face had changed from the first time that he had seen me in the emergency room. Two weeks had passed and the other doctor couldn't do anything with my broken cheekbone because I was in a coma. My husband vividly remembers the doctors joking and checking on him to make sure he was alright.

The surgery left a slight disfiguration on my right cheek. One of my doctors asked me if I wanted to have plastic surgery to have the disfiguration removed. I was already so thankful for what the Lord had already done for me. I felt like the slight scar was as significant to me as the rainbow was to Noah after the flood. This would always be a sign of what the Lord had done for me. Therefore I said I would just keep it.

**What About the Children**

Unfortunately, the children responded in a different manner to my physical appearance. Whenever certain children would walk pass me or I would wait in line, they would point in my direction, stare at me, or move closer to the adults. The care-giver would often pull them closer to them and say, "It's not polite to stare" or with a slight tug they would say, "Come here and turn around." I know children mean well and children will be children. This is to say that children are usually honest and blunt with their feelings. Often people shy away from people or things that they don't understand. Nevertheless, the stares and the turning away hurt and were painful.

My self-centered pity was short lived as my passion and dedication for the education of the children prevailed. I wanted to get back to doing what I enjoyed doing and that was teaching. I felt strong enough to return to work. Even though I always worked with the children in the church, I knew that it wasn't a good idea to try to teach both the children at school, and the children from the church at this particular time. Because of the severity of the car accident, I had to have a CAT scan to prove that I was competent to teach again. This procedure would ensure that the students would continue to receive a quality education. I said okay.

## I'm Back

After a lot of determination, hard work, and the needed medical documentation required by the school board, I returned to work in the Fall of that school year (1990-91). However, I didn't return to the fourth grade classroom, I was placed in Chapter-One. I was hired as a Chapter-One Computer Reading-lab Teacher. At first, I was hurt about loosing my classroom but I realized that this was an opportunity where I could still teach.

Everyone was astonished to see me comprehending and getting along as if nothing had ever happened to me. Reflecting back, I remember the loving support that I received from my co-workers. This same type of support was reciprocated with my husband as well as with my friends. Nevertheless, I felt imprisoned by the extra support and the over protectiveness. Many people treated me as if I had a deformity or as if I was glass and would break.

I would share the revelation with my co-workers, family and friends of how the Lord desires to bless us according to His riches and glory. But the jealousy that we hold in our hearts towards others and the way we talk about each other in a negative way behind each other's backs is one reason why our blessings are withheld. I noticed that people would quickly say, "Okay, and I'll see you later", or they would look at me with a raised eyebrow and slowly change the subject. However, most people were very careful about what they said or did around me.

My attention turned from the adults to the melancholy look in the children's eyes or to their tender cries. The tender cries of the children manifested themselves in the form of anger, loudness, and in various degrees of disrespect.

**Can Anybody Hear Me**

It's funny how I could hear the children very clearly. I could feel their pain and I didn't want them to feel rejected any longer. Oddly enough, it seemed as if being placed in the Chapter-One-Computer Reading Lab was the best thing that could have happened to me. I felt my purpose and could see that I was making a difference.

The students who were placed in Chapter-One were the students who received a certain score in Reading and in Math in the annual Iowa Test of Basic Skills (ITBS) test that was given system-wide to the students in grades one through twelve in each school. They were considered to be "At risk." That meant they may not succeed in the regular classroom setting. Therefore they were allowed to go into the Chapter-One-Computer Reading or Math lab to receive additional help.

Instead of having 18-26 students, I had about 80 students reading on the lowest reading level. Twelve to sixteen students were taught in the lab during a setting. I had six periods of reading students on at least five different reading levels. Thus, programs and an Individualized Educational Plan (IEP) had to be written to meet each student's needs. Students were administered tests on a regular basis and Permanent record's folders were kept on each one of them. The student's loved it. They were good students and did great work. All they wanted was for someone to stop long enough to listen and to show that they cared. Many times their writing exceeded that of some of the students in the regular classrooms. **I'm a living witness that God will hear your cry and then give you exactly what you need.**

## Guiding Principles/Supportive Scriptures

- He staggered not at the promise of God through unbelief; but was strong in faith, giving glory to God; and being fully persuaded, that what He had promised, He was able to perform. Romans 4:20 (KJV)

- I have come to know God as Jehovah-Raphael/ Repheka. The Lord is my Healer. [14]

- And when Jesus heard that, He said, "This sickness is not unto death, but for the glory of God, that the Son of God might be glorified thereby. John 11:4 (KJV)

- That your faith should not stand in the wisdom of men, but in the power of God, I Corinthians 2:5.

- For we walk by faith and not by sight. II Corinthians 5:7 (KJV)

- For we are saved by hope; but hope that is seen is not hope; for what a man seeth, why doth he yet hope for? But if we hope for that we see not, then do we with patience wait for it. Romans 8:24-25 (KJV)

- The righteous cry and the Lord heareth, and delivereth them out of all their troubles, Psalm 34:17. In the day when I cried Thou answeredst me, and strengthenedst me with strength in my soul. Psalms 138:3 (KJV)

- Whose adorning let it not be that outward adorning of plaiting the hair, and of wearing of gold or of putting on of apparel; But let it be the hidden man of the heart, in that which is not corruptible, even the ornament of a meek and quiet spirit, which in the sight of God of great price. I Peter 3:3-4 (KJV)

**Let Us Pray:**

Father, in the Mighty name of Jesus, I pray that You will forgive me for my sins and short comings. I want to thank You. Thank You for hearing my cry. Thank You for knowing my name. I believe that Your Word is true. I pray that others will believe that Jesus is the Son of God and has power to save. May Your children be restored in every area that they need. In Jesus' name I pray, amen.

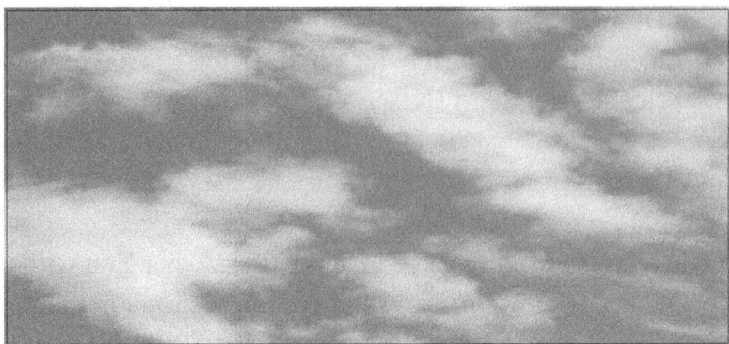

## Chapter Six

*For this cause shall a man leave*
*his father and mother,*
*and shall be joined unto his wife,*
*and they two shall be one*
Ephesians 5:31 (KJV)

# The Two Shall Be One Flesh

Let me say that during all of this time, my husband never looked at me as though anything different had happened to my face. *Thank you John, I will always love you for that!* I became pregnant that same year and again John and I were delighted. Three months later, I had a miscarriage. My body wasn't strong enough yet to carry a baby. The doctor advised me not to have another child right now because he said that it would be too much trauma on my body.

I remember feeling such a sense of loss. Yet, I thought that I would only need a couple of days from work to recuperate. My husband, however, requested that I take a week off from work, so I did. It wasn't until the end of the week, on Friday, that the reality of the loss really hit me. That morning I tried to get out of bed, but I couldn't stop crying. I remember blaming myself for losing the baby and asking God to forgive me for doing too much too soon.

John had to remind me that both of us had lost a child. My husband wasn't accustomed to talking about his feelings, but finally he said, "Lores, it wasn't just you who lost this baby. We both lost the baby. I wanted this baby as much as you did. I'm hurting too."

I sat up and said, "I'm sorry baby; I didn't realize that I was shutting you out of the grieving process."

Both of us believed in our heart that this baby was going to be a girl and it was. This was later confirmed by the doctor to be true. Somehow, with the help of God, John and I got through this crisis by embracing each other and holding on to what we had, our love for each other and John Jr. **I'm a living witness that God will bring you through any loss.** The most important thing is not to get stuck in one place and with the help of God; be able to move on.

I've heard different people use Scripture to try to ease the pain and console a person experiencing the loss of a child. Scripture is true and we know that God's Word changes not, however, some Scriptures can hurt more than heal when used out of context. For example, "All things work together for the good to them that love God, to them who are called according to His purpose" Romans 8:28 (KJV). I don't know how loosing our baby could work for our good, but I know that God knows. If anyone says anything that hurts your feeling instead of helping you to feel comfort, remember to forgive them. Most people are unsure about what to say. I've found that sometimes all a person need is to know that you are there for them, or for you to look at them with loving eyes and listen to them, lend a shoulder to cry on, or give any support that they may need. It's called the **Ministry of Presence**; just be there.

## Your Loving Eyes

Your loving eyes and smile is what attracted me to you twenty–four years ago. As I scan through the pages of my mind, I quietly watched as the pages stopped and my eyes focused on the year of 1983. I was twenty-three years old and I was determined not to meet any young men, while I traveled, so I had the ticket agent pre-print my ticket which showed each city where the bus would stop and the number of days that I planned to stay in each city. I thought that was a good plan, however, it wasn't God's plan.

The day I got to Albany, Georgia, a friend of the family saw me at my Aunt Bernice and Uncle C's house. He told John Floyd that I was back in town. John and I first met when we were teenagers, while I was visiting for my summer vacation. The next, day John came to my family's house to see me. It was then that I heard the faint words, *"This is going to be your husband."* Needless-to-say, we have been together every since.

## I Do...I will

"... Will thou have this man to be thy lawful wedded husband, to live together after God's ordinance, in the holy estate of matrimony?" I faintly heard the minister as he was saying these words.

Time just seemed like it froze, and all I could see was John; Mr. Tall, Dark, and handsome in a white tuxedo that was tailored to fit. He was captivating. *I looked at my mother and thought, Jesus, I'm so glad that she could come to be in the wedding. I needed to see her face. My sister Belinda and my friend Pam also came from Pennsylvania to be in the wedding. Daddy was not able to come, so my uncle C walked me down the aisle. My Italian colleague and friend, Laurie who was like a sister to me came down from New Jersey. I was so nervous.* I noticed that the flowers that I was holding were shaking. *We had been planning this wedding for over a year and it was hard to believe that the day was finally here. John was adamant about not setting a wedding date until he got a job. He had just gotten laid-off from his previous job before I returned to Albany. I could still hear concerned family and friends near and far asking, "Lores, ya'll still getting married? What's taking so long?"*

The minister continued, "Will thou obey him and serve him, love honor, and keep him in sickness and in health; and, forsaking all others, keep thee only unto him, so long as ye both shall live (Hiscox, 1984)? [15]"

As I looked into his loving eyes, he smiled at me and I replied, "Yes, I do; I mean I will."

After the excitement of the wedding died down, the honeymoon was over, and the gifts were placed in their respective places; reality set in. By this I mean the money had to be budgeted and some money had to be saved. Then there was the issue of being left alone and not knowing where the other spouse was. The bed had to be made up daily, the top put back on the toothpaste, the toilet seat being left up, putting the toilet paper on the spool backwards, socks and shoes being left in the middle of the floor, clothes that were taken off were left on the bedroom chair, the clothes had to be washed or taken out of the basket and put away. Dinner had to be cooked ever day. Paper or books were on the table, keeping the bedroom dresser from being messy, dirty dishes left in the sink, or having a messy house none of that was discussed before we got married. I didn't know what to expect! But I found out in a hurry. The honeymoon was definitely over!!!

Moreover, John and I were as different as day and night. He was very talkative and I was very shy at that time. He was an extrovert and I was an introvert. He was flashy and daring, I was reserved and conservative. John was from the South and had a southern drawl; I was from the North and was called a Yankee with an accent by some. John spoke slowly while I spoke faster. I was an educator and John was a challenge to all of his teachers. John was right-handed and I was left-handed.

Let me make it clear that I'm not emphasizing that any of these traits are better or worse than the other; just differences and those were the facts.

John and I didn't have pre-marital counseling. So I wondered how we were going to bring two different cultural backgrounds and personality types together to become one flesh. It would take God's divine help, lots of patience and hard work on our parts. As with anything you try to build, the foundation should be with God, if you want it to stand. Plus I didn't really know that becoming one flesh meant the consummation of the marriage.

Psalms 127: 1 says, "Except the Lord builds the house, they labor in vain that build it."

Earlier, I forgot the most important difference between us; John didn't go to church. He was a good man but he only went to church on special occasions. John was brought up going to church just as I was, but he stopped going to church when he got older and went into the military.

## The Unbelieving Spouse

The Scripture states that all have sinned and come short of His glory (Romans 3:23, KJV). Since I knew that I was a sinner saved by grace, I am by no means casting stones or judging another. Matthew 7:1 says "Judge not that ye be not judged."

It is written in I John 1:8-9 (KJV).
*"If we say that we have no sin, we deceive ourselves, and the truth is not in us. If we confess our sins, He is faithful and just to forgive us our sins, and to cleanse us from all unrighteousness."* I'm not saying that John didn't believe in God, he just didn't go to church. As a result, I would have to take John Jr. to church alone. I knew that John loved me and his son. I also knew that I could depend on him if I needed anything. After a while that just wasn't enough. I sensed a need for the man of the house to be the Spiritual Priest that he was ordained to be.

Paul stated in *Romans 10:1 (KJV)*: *"Brethren, my heart's desire and prayer to God for Israel is that they might be saved."*

I've learned that It doesn't matter how nice, kind, or sweet you are, if you haven't accepted Jesus Christ as your personal Savior, you will not be saved and go to heaven. [16]

This seems like such a hard statement to make, especially since salvation is free. Salvation is as simple as confessing with your mouth and believing in your heart.
It is written in Romans 10:9 (KJV):

> "…If thou shalt confess with thy mouth the Lord Jesus, and shalt believe in thy heart that God hath raised Him from the dead, thou shalt be saved."

I also knew that the wife or husband could stand in the gap for the unbelieving spouse. Therefore, I held fast to the Scripture in *I Peter3:1-2* (KJV) which states:

> *"Likewise, ye wives be in subjection to your own husbands; if any obey not the Word,   they may without the Word be won by the conversation of the wives; while they behold your chaste conversation coupled with fear."*

Moreover, this similar feeling is expressed in I Corinthians 7:14 (KJV). However, in this Scripture, Paul explained the importance of either believing spouse upholding this Scripture as he states: "…Else were your children unclean, but now are they holy."

## The Closed Chapters

As with every marriage, there are closed chapters that are between only husband, wife, and God. I remember trying everything that I knew to bring John back into the church; but nothing seemed to work. I even tried to change and do some of the things that he liked to do or go to some of the places that he liked to go. I went to some house parties and had a New Year's Toast on several days besides having one on New Year's Eve or on our anniversary night.

When I was growing up I used to go to parties and was called "Dancing D", but I knew that I didn't want to pick up old habits that I had already put down.

There were times when both of us wanted to leave or we wanted the other people to leave. Finally both of us declared that neither of us was going anywhere anymore.

We are also blessed because neither of our parents entered into our marriage and took sides. Both of us knew that we were loved as a natural child, not just as a son-in-law or as a daughter-in-law.

My mother always reminded me before she passed, "You got to be careful not to tell other women or people in the street what goes on in your house." She reminded me, "As soon as you give up on your man they will be the main ones that will be there to grab him."

My dad, on the other hand, cautioned me as he lowered his voice to almost a whisper, "If you ever leave home, your home will never be the same when you come back. Not only that but, you will not be able to work out any differences that the two of you may have had." Dad ended by stating, "When you feel like you can't take any more, take a little more."

Being a deacon, at that time, Dad would always direct me to the Scriptures. So I searched the Scriptures to see what was written in the Scriptures.

## What Would Jesus Do

According to Titus 2:2-6 (KJV), aged woman were to live in such a way that was fitting for someone serving the

Lord (not speaking bad about others or being a heavy drinker) so that they could instruct and train the younger woman how to be sober, and to love their own husbands and children, how to keep harmony and take care of the home, and how to be obedient to their own husbands. Likewise, the older men were to live in such a way that would bring respect, being sober, having integrity, patience, self control, faith, and wisdom. The young men were to be encouraged to imitate this same pattern of behavior.

Marriage is a constitution of God (Hiscox, 1968 p.199).[17] We are commanded to submit ourselves one to another in the fear of God. This can be examined in the fifth chapter of Ephesians where Christ became the joining force. In this chapter, the woman is admonished to submit and be in subjection unto her own husband as the church is to submit and be in subjection unto Christ in everything. We are reminded that the husband is the head of his wife as Christ is the head of the Church.

Moreover, the husbands are instructed to love their wives as their own bodies and as Christ also loved the church. The Scripture points out the fact that no man hates his own body; but nourishes and takes care of it. Just as Christ nourishes and takes care of the church. This is the reason why a man is supposed to leave his father and mother and be joined unto his wife. **Thus, the two shall become one flesh.** The Bible points out that this is a great mystery. Nevertheless, the man is to love the wife as he would love himself and the woman is to reverence her husband.

We are reminded by Jesus, in Matthew 19:8 (KJV), that Moses permitted a bill of divorce because of the hardness of men and woman's hearts. However, it was not God's intention for us to be divorced in the beginning. In addition to this, verse 9, in that same chapter says," A man who divorces his wife and marries another, commits adultery; unless she has been unfaithful. A similar statement like this can be found in Deuteronomy 24:1-4 (KJV), except in this chapter, the female may go and marry another man; if she is given a bill of divorce. However, if the second husband divorces her or dies, the former husband can not take her again to be his wife. This would now be considered an abomination; which means a feeling of extreme disgust or dislike (Merriam-Webster, 1988), unto the Lord because the woman was now considered defiled, impure, or unclean (NLB).

This restriction was to prevent casual remarriage because it was not to be taken lightly the first time (The Life Application Study Bible, (1996). Marriage was meant to be an eternal state and divorce a permanent state. Through the years, I found that you can't change anyone. Only God can change the heart of man. When we have gone as far as we can go, that is when we need to reach out for spiritual help and guidance. I can remember getting annoyed when a former church member, named Louise, would always stand up and say to the church, "I learned to Let Go and Let God." I would say to myself, *that doesn't even make sense. "Let go and let God." Let go of what and "Let God what?"*

**Let Go and Let God**

Finally, I just gave up and said, "Lord, I'm tired. I'm tired of praying and fasting for my husband's salvation. I'm not going to worry about this anymore. This is Your child and I give him to You." I forgot that I couldn't save anyone.

I couldn't pin God into a time frame in granting my request. That would have been unreasonable on my part and so unfair.

When I let go and gave the situation to God, I heard these words in my spirit, *"I was waiting for you to let go and let Me do it;"* It was a still quiet voice in my spirit.

The Scripture forewarns us not to be weary in well doing (II Thessalonians 3:13 KJV). We are encouraged that if we faint not, we shall reap in due season (Galatians 5:4 KJV). When I stopped worrying about the situation and started concentrating on Jesus things started happening. There is a song that says, "And if I, if I be lifted up from the earth, I'll draw all men unto Me." **I'm a living witness that statement is true.** In 1992, I joined the church that the majority of my husband's family belonged to because we started going to church as a family.

## Guiding Principles/Supportive Scriptures

- For this cause shall a man leave his father and mother, and shall be joined unto his wife, and they two shall be one flesh. Ephesians 5:31 (KJV)

- I have come to know God as Jehovah-Shamah; the Lord is There.[18]

- Submitting yourselves one to another in the fear of God. Wives, submit yourselves unto your own husbands, as unto the Lord. Ephesians 5: 21-22 (KJV)

- For the husband is the head of the wife, even as Christ is the head of the church; and He is the savior of the body...Ephesians 5:23 (KJV)

- So ought men to love their wives as their own bodies. He that loveth his wife loveth himself. Ephesians 5:28 (KJV)

- Likewise, wives, be in subjection to your own husbands; that, if any obey not the Word, they may without the Word be won by the conversation of the wife. I Peter 3:1 (KJV)

- That if thou shall confess with thy mouth the Lord Jesus, and shall believe in thine heart that God has raised Him from the dead, thou shall be saved. Romans 10:9 (KJV)

- And let us not be weary in well doing: for in due season we shall reap, if we faint not. Galatians 6:9 (KJV)

**Let Us Pray:**

Father, in the Mighty name of *Jesus,* I pray that You forgive me for all of my sins and short comings. I thank You for my husband. I pray for husbands and wives everywhere. Help us as wives to submit to our husbands, as unto the Lord and help husbands to honor their wives, so that their prayers will not be hindered. In Jesus' name I pray, amen.

## Chapter Seven

*We are troubled on every side, yet not distressed,
perplexed, yet not in despair, persecuted, but not forsaken,
cast down, but not destroyed.*
II Corinthians 4:8-9

# From Trials to Triumphs

I am so thankful that John and I didn't get stuck in
our loss. However, I did want to have another baby so
that John Jr. wouldn't be an only child. My prayer was
answered on June 6, 1993. The Lord blessed us with a
baby girl who weighed 9 lbs and 1 ounce. We named her
Davina (the beloved one) Jonette Floyd. Lord, thank
You, for giving us another child. In January of 1994, I
enrolled at the University to work on a Master's Degree
in School Counseling. I felt that I had finally met my
destiny. Little did I know that the Lord was preparing
me to handle the next miracle. On July 7 [th] of the same
year, the Flint River overflowed and much of Albany,
Georgia was flooded.

# The Flood of 1994

Thinking back on that day, I remember that I had just finished washing two loads of clothes and I placed the two baskets in the trunk of the car. I planned to dry the clothes at the Laundromat after John came home from work. *"Lord, I sure will be glad when You bless us with another dryer. I don't want You to think that I'm not thankful; I can remember the times when we didn't have a washer or dryer. After all that You have brought us through, I know that this too shall pass."* I went back to the kitchen table where I was working on a research paper and on other assignments for the classes that I was taking during the summer term. The telephone started ringing so I stopped working to answer it.

My cousin Leonard who lived down the street was on the line, "You got your things put up or packed?'

I could hear the alarm and concern in his voice; he knew that I usually had the radio on listening to gospel music. "My things put up or packed? Leonard, what are you talking about?"

He said, "You haven't been watching the news?" We've already started putting some things up high and we're going to go over to our sister Roni's house. Do you want to come with us?"

"I don't think so "cuz", I told him. I knew there were at least five family members (uncle C, aunt Bernice, Lenard, Jackie, Sherneka, and Antwon) going from his house plus the three of us. That would have been too many in a house that already had three people, Mitch, Roni, and DeeDee, living there. Thank you for checking on me. I'm going to turn on the television and call John. I told him I'd call him back if I needed him."

I went to the living room and turned on the television. The news was about Topical Storm Alberto, which had come ashore off the coast of Florida and how the direction of the flooding was so unpredictable because it kept changing its course. Warnings were being made for the different counties. Everyone was asked to stay tuned to the news in case they had to evacuate.

Immediately, I called John at work and shared what cousin Leonard said and what I had heard on the television.

John said, "Baby, when it rains like this, the most we usually get is some water on J Street. Everything should be okay," but keep the television on and it shouldn't be too long before I'll be able to come home.

I said, "Okay"

"What are the children doing?"

I said Little Man (John Jr.) was watching television in the living room before I turned the channel to the news and Davina was in her walker with me.

"Okay, I'm going to finish up this paper work and get ready to come home.

I said, "Okay, I'll see you when you get here," and hung up the phone.

I started getting Little Man and Davina dressed and fed. I put Davina back in her walker while I packed her baby bag with pampers, baby food, bottles, and some clothes. I thought to myself, I sure don't want anything to happen to this research paper and my *other class-work. Just in case, I better pack it all in my school bag and put it up high so nothing can get to it.* While I was putting the baby's bag and my school bag on a high dresser in Little Man's room, I heard someone knocking at the front screen door.

"Just a minute," I said.

When I walked into the living room, I saw my sister-in-law, Barbra Jenkins at the door. "What are you doing here?" I asked.

"I went to class but they closed the technical school because of the flooding in some counties. The roads weren't safe. Drivers were cautioned not to drive across roads filled with water and some students had to drive long distances to get to class. I just stopped by to check and make sure that you and the children were alright. You and the children are welcome to come over to my house if you want to."

I said, "That's sweet sis, but we're going to wait until John comes home."

"Okay, if you change your mine, you know you're welcomed."

## The First Evacuation

It wasn't long after my sister-in-law left that John came home. After speaking to everyone, he went into the bedroom to change clothes. When he came out of the bedroom, Little Man came running out of the kitchen screaming, "Daddy, Daddy; what's all that water doing in the back yard?"

John went into the kitchen and looked out of the opened screened back door that led to the backyard and then he shouted, "Lores get the baby and let's go!"

I got the baby and went into Little Man's bedroom to get the baby's bag and my school bag; then I ran out to the car where John Sr. and Little Man were in the front yard. The water had started coming down the street and was about an inch high as we got into the car.

John backed out of the driveway and started driving the car down the street. Before we could get half-way down the street, the water came so fast that the tires could not stay on the road. The car started floating. Little Man saw all the water that was around him outside the window of the car and some that had started coming through the floor of the car. He started crying and screaming with a sharp piercing sound; then the baby started crying because her brother was crying.

All of a sudden, there were about six men surrounding the car and they started pushing it to the end of the street and onto the street that was adjacent to it. That part of the street was slightly elevated. It was not a low area so there was no water on the ground on that side. We got out of the car and I sat Little Man on top of the car as I held Davina and consoled both of them. John went back to the street to help the other men push the cars that had gotten stuck in the water.

When John came back to the car his pants were wet from the knees down. He asked if we were alright. I told him we were okay.

John looked inside the car and said, "The water drained out of the car; come on, let's get the children back in the car and drive over to my sister Gloria's house.

John turned the key and the car started. "Thank You Jesus!" was all that I could say. We drove to his sister's house, which was about ten minutes away. We rang the doorbell and his sister answered the door and said, "Lord, look at my babies." She took little Man's hand and said, "Ya'll come on in."

The television was on, and every station was talking about the flood and giving the predictions about the paths of the water, the destruction that had already been done and news about how some people had to get rescued by boat from their homes. A Warning was issued for anyone caught looting (stealing merchandise because of a natural disaster) and a curfew was given for children and teenagers to be off the streets from dusk to dawn. Everyone was asked to be ready to evacuate their homes on a moment's notice, if a fireman or Police Officers told them to do so.

I just watched the television in amazement and held my children close to me. I thought to myself, "How did I manage to escape the 1977 flood that occurred in my home town of Johnstown, Pennsylvania." I was visiting my sister Belinda at Penn State University when it occurred. It was a blessing that we were able to get back into the city of Johnstown. It was because we volunteered to help clean up. It was amazing how I missed that flood, but now here I was in the middle of a flood in Albany, Georgia.

John said, "I remember, I was stationed in Germany, when I heard about the flood in your hometown. My sergeant let me call Johnstown to see if you and your family were alright."

My sister-in-law interrupted saying "You know you can stay with me." She had two children and her grand-daughter staying with her, Milton her nineteen-year-old son, his daughter, MyShyia, who was thirteen months old, and ShaNovia her fifteen year-old daughter (4 people plus the four of us). She said we could sleep in her bedroom and she would sleep on the couch in the living room. It was amazing how people were willing to help each other.

"Did you get a chance to save anything?" I guess she was wondering about the clothes.

I explained why I had two baskets of clothes in the car. "You're welcome to use my dryer,"she said. She asked John to get the baskets of clothes out of the car. He brought the baskets in the house and I put them in the dryer.

Most of the evening was spent calling family members on the telephone to see how they were doing, watching the news, and talking to each other. We ate dinner, being thankful most of all that we still had our lives. I folded the clothes and put them in the basket and placed the basket in the bedroom where we would be sleeping. The four of us slept together on a waterbed.

## The Second Evacuation

After our second night, shortly after we woke up and got dressed, a fireman knocked on the door and told us that we had to evacuate. The flood waters were beginning to slowly fill the trenches that were behind or beside certain houses in the neighborhood. Reluctantly but quickly, we gathered our two baskets while my sister-in-law and her children packed some clothes in a suitcase and we headed to his other sister's house. She was the oldest one in the family.

When we got to John's other sister Barbara's house, you could look at her face and see that she had mixed emotions. She was glad to see us and to know that we were safe; however, she knew that seeing us meant that we had been told to evacuate.

"Come on in, we just got to find a place for ya'll to put your things and sleep."

There were fifteen people by now. My sister-in-law asked my husband and our nephew to help take a mattress off one of the beds, and directed them to put it in the hallway that led to the living room and to the front entrance of the house that had a screened in porch. This was the designated place where my family was to sleep. The mattress was wider than the hallway so part of it turned upright on the wall. I sat our two baskets of clothes in the corner of the hall leading to the outside door where there would be no traffic.

## The Extended Family

There were twenty-three people living in the house: mother-in-law, men, (dads, brothers, and brother-in-laws) women (mothers, sisters, and sister-in-laws), teenagers (sisters, brother, cousin), boys, girls, and babies. We were like packed sardines in a can. It was uncomfortable but amazingly, it worked. I guess it worked because we were in the survival mode and it had to work. Nevertheless, I saw how an **extended family** can work.

In spite of the devastation, business as usual or as much as possible had to continue. We didn't need an alarm clock because someone was always awake or moving around.

Some of the women worked together to cook the meals, some women made sure the smaller children were alright, others handled any arguments, while one or two always listened to what was being said on the news about the flood. The children, who were first cousins, were not bored because they had plenty of company. They played games and made their own fun. The men would walk or drive around and check out how things looked in the neighborhood. They especially kept or paid close attention to how high the waters were filling up in the trenches near the house where we were staying. This information would get reported upon their return, and we would talk about what we would do if we had to evacuate again.

I knew that this was a mighty act and only God could deliver us and bring restoration. We needed God to deliver us just like He delivered Moses at the Red Sea. [19]

Isaiah 59:19 (KJV) tells us, "When the enemy shall come in like a flood, the Spirit of the Lord will lift up a standard again him." That standard is the Word of God. *James 5:13 (KJBV) says, "Is there any among you afflicted? Let him pray."* "Yes, it's praying time!" I said softly.

## My Prayer Closet

"It's praying time." I said again, only louder this time. I asked my sister-in-law if I could read her Bible.

"It sure is praying time," she said as she got up and brought a Bible back to the kitchen table. I opened the Bible to one of my favorite Scriptures, Isaiah 43 and I read verse two out loud:

"When thou passest through the waters, I will be with thee
And through the rivers, they shall not overflow thee:
When thou walkest through the fire, thou shall not be burnt,
Neither shall the flame kindle upon thee."
We joined hands and had a family prayer:

*Father God, in the name of Jesus, we come to You. We want to thank You for keeping us safe and we pray for the safety for others in the city. Forgive us for our sins and short comings. Lord, we know that You have all power in Your hands. We lift up these words found in Isaiah 43:2 back to you in prayer, and we know that You are not a man that You should lie or the son of man that You should repent. Look down on the city of Albany and have mercy,Lord. If you leave us, whether shall we go? Lift up Your mighty hand, we pray, and bring the waters under control again. We bind up the spirit of fear and loose the spirit of courage.* I felt someone nudge my side and squeeze my hand and one of the children started crying so I decided to end the prayer *in Jesus' name we pray amen.*

I left the Bible opened on the table and read that Scripture daily so I could hide these words in my heart and gain strength. I knew we would get through this and that everything was going to be alright.

The extended family got the best of almost everyone, after a couple of days. You couldn't enjoy the luxury of several things that we so often took for granted, such as, having a lot of room, having privacy, not having to rush in the bathroom, watching what you wanted on television, having peace and quiet (unless it was very late at night), taking a nap, having leftovers, cooking what you wanted to eat, going shopping, and going to church. Not having some of these luxuries caused the family to react in different ways.

My sister-in-law got one of her brothers to go with her to see if there was any damage to her house. When they got there, she was relieved to discover that everything was fine. The flood waters only reached the street where her house was located. Some of the other houses on the lower end of the neighborhood did get flooded.

The fire department gave her the okay to return home. My sister-in-law, Gloria, returned to the house and started packing her clothes and told her children to get their clothes together.

"I wonder when we will get the okay to return to our house," I said feeling a little melancholy. I was happy for my sister-in-law, but like Dorothy in the Wizard of Oz (I thought to myself), *"There's no place like home" and I wanted to go home. Only, I didn't have a home to go to anymore.*

"Lores, you, John and the children can come back to my house and stay with us if you want."

We said okay. John got the two baskets and I got the baby's bag. I left my school bag in the car because the university where I attended had flooded and I wouldn't need it.

## Business As Usual

We returned to Gloria's house thankful that we had our own bedroom to sleep in again. I thought that it would be nice when we could sleep in that waterbed again. Those few nights, everyone rolled on me and the weight pinned my arm on the side board. It didn't matter how I shifted around; the results would be the same. I would think, *how can you complain about this? There were people who were in worse conditions. I still had a lot to be thankful for.* I would constantly remind myself by saying these words, *"and this too shall pass."*

There were so many people worst off than we were. Many people had to evacuate with no place to go. Several churches, schools, and play ground recreational centers opened their doors. We watched the news all day every day since that was the quickest way to get updated information. It was predicted that the flood waters would crest at forty feet. The news also showed the height of the flood waters in some houses. People were standing in water that was waist deep. Volunteers were racing to fill sand bags in an attempt to save the college located by the river and the Civic Center. People were getting rescued in motor boats. Many pets were found and saved too. It was reported that five people from Albany, GA were killed as a direct result of the flood. The flood waters forced 400 caskets out of the graves in the two cemeteries nearest the river. President Clinton declared the city of Albany a state of emergency (Flood Watch '94). [20]

Therefore, Federal Emergency Management Association (FEMA) was called in for assistance. The Red Cross also aided in anyway they could. Help was now available for getting assistance to supply basic needs such as food, clothing vouchers, food stamps, housing, and health care. There was, however, a long waiting list to receive a FEMA Trailer. You also had to be willing and patient and stand in line to receive any benefits or supplies for your home. I would have "Little Man by one hand, Davina by the other hand, with her baby bag filled with snacks for Little Man on my shoulder. We would wait in line until we got what we needed for our family. If Davina got sleepy I would hold her or sometimes we would be able to sit in a chair until our number was called.

Paperwork had to be filled out and information was given in order to receive different services.

I thought about the Scripture found in Isaiah 50:7 (KJV), which says,

*"For the Lord God will help me therefore shall I not be confounded: Therefore have I set my face like a flint, and I know that I shall not be ashamed.* I would say to myself, *This too shall pass.*

The clean up process was being done in the city of Albany and the people's basic needs were being attended to. I thank the Lord that I packed my school work in my schoolbag because classes resumed as if nothing had happened; other than the university forming a partnership with a high school to continue classes. I am blessed that I did not have to ask for an extension on any papers that were due. John continued to work on his job and also got another job as a Security Officer for the night. I continued to help my sister-in-law with the cooking and washing the dishes. I would walk the children and my niece to the playground during the early evening to give them a change to release built up energy. It also gave me a chance to relieve my own built-up stress. During the night, I would work on my college assignments.

As the days passed, John drove to the area of town where we lived, to see if we could get back into our house. This was the second time he had gone to survey the damage (the first time was when we evacuated and went to his oldest sister's house). I thought about Noah and the flood and got my Bible. I read in Genesis chapter eight how Noah sent a raven and a dove to see if the waters were dried up from the earth. The dove returned to the ark because it could find no rest for her feet, but the raven did not return until the waters were dried up.

The flood waters had receded; however, we still could not return to our home on our street until the property authorities had gone through all the houses and made sure they were safe to enter. John returned to his sister's house and said, "Lores, you'll never guess what I found."

I met him in the kitchen and said "what?"
He held up a bird cage and said, "Mr. Birdie."

I forgot all about our indoor pet; Mr. Birdie. When I shouted, "Mr. Birdie," the children came running into the kitchen and started jumping up and down and they joined in and said "Mr. Birdie, Mr. Birdie."

I told Mr. Birdie, that I was sorry that I had forgotten him. In retrospect, I remember taking Mr. Birdie's cage off of the kitchen table and placing it back on the washing machine after I put the two baskets of clothes in the trunk of the car. Lord, I thank You for guiding my actions and for giving us another reason to have hope.

**New Hope**

The proper authorities finally gave the okay for us to go into our homes and savage what ever we could. When John and I walked through the house together, it felt as though I was walking in a dream. Everything that we had saved and bought for nine years was ruined or destroyed. Some framed pictures were saved that were hung high on the wall.

However, very few items were saved because of the mildew and the unsanitary conditions that resulted after the flood waters receded. Everyone was asked to get a tetanus shot. We lost our home and 90% of our possessions, but Praise God, we still had our lives. We were devastated, to say the least. It felt as though someone had pulled the rug from under our feet. This lost was painful. Moreover, it made the period of recuperating from my car accident seem like it was nothing.

When it was time for school to begin, provisions were made for several of the schools that were flooded to accommodate the teachers and students. One of the basic skills of life was implemented, that was sharing. I had to share the Reading Computer Lab with another teacher who had to bring her students to the lab too. As we shared the Computer Reading lab, we also had to share the Teacher's Aid. We found we each had something to offer the other. Needless to say, new friendships were birthed. However, it was a hard and trying time for everyone; having to live with so many adults in the workplace as well as in the home. This situation tested all our patience. Time passed and two weeks turned into two months and counting.

I prayed about it. The Bibles says in Isaiah 65:24 (KJV), "And it shall come to pass, that before they call, I will answer; and while they are yet speaking, I will hear." And He did.

John called his great Aunt Shelma (now deceased) who was around 79 years old and lived alone. He asked if she would let our family stay with her while we waited for a FEMA Trailer. She gladly accepted, because we needed her and she really needed us too. The four of us still had to sleep together, but this bed had a regular mattress. Praise the Lord, no more pain. This also gave the children and me an opportunity to get to know our great aunt better.

## Temporary New Home

Three days later, we were enthusiastic when we received a call informing us that a FEMA trailer was ready for us and we could move in. "Halleluiah, thank You Lord." was all that I could say. Isaiah 40:31 (KJV) say,

"But they that wait upon the Lord shall renew their strength; they shall mount up with wings as eagles; they shall run, and not be weary; and they shall walk, and not faint."

We gathered what belongings we had and shed tears of joy, appreciation, and thanksgiving for her hospitality. Then we left to move into our own new temporary home.

Shortly after that, the Program in which I had been hired to work closed. The Chapter One Program was implemented in some of the schools to include all the students. "I thank God!" I know that God never closes one door without opening up another. In 1995, I was given an opportunity to teach in a second grade classroom. This time, however, another second grade teacher had to share her classroom with my students and me until more FEMA trailers were provided for classroom space.

It has been said you should be careful how you treat people, because you never know when you will need someone or something. Then there is the golden rule that says treat others the way that you would like to be treated. However, the Scripture in Matthew 7:2 says "…And with what measure you mete, it shall be measured to you again." With respect, cooperation, flexibility, and a lot of communication, the merger worked.

I observed and learned a style of teaching and techniques from a veteran teacher and she learned a different style of teaching and techniques demonstrated by me. Approximately a month later my students and I were able to move into our own classroom.

In 1998, we experienced another flood.[21] The city however, was more prepared this time so, not as much damage was done. The following year, I was hired as a School Counselor at another elementary school. I felt like I had met my purpose and was making a difference with the students. A highlight of this job was working with the Student Council members. The Student Council members were required to do a service project each month to help develop their character in the area of helps and service. At least once a year the students would make cards and take a field trip to the nursing home. We would sing songs, read stories and share cards with the patients to help brighten their day. Some patients who were slumped over or left to sit alone in the break room would slowly lift their heads and begin to sit up, while other patients' eyes would light up remembering when…, or smile with adoration and appreciation. Giving back to their response, the students embraced their friendly gestures and it made them feel like they had really made a difference in the lives of the patients.

## God Won't Put More on You Than You Can Bear

God is so wonderful and magnificent. It is amazing how He strategically orchestrates our lives. During November of 1999, my dad, who lives in Johnstown, PA., called to tell me mom was in the hospital. Mom had to go to the hospital a lot lately because of her illnesses. Therefore I asked my dad, if he thought I needed to come home.

He sighed and said, "I'm going to leave that up to you. The doctor wanted me to let everyone know how serious her condition was."

We had a prayer together and I told dad that I would call him the next day, after I had an opportunity to speak with my Principal. Based on the situation I knew I needed to go home.

That night, I had a dream that left such a strong impression on me that I woke up saying and knowing without a shadow of a doubt that, *God will put no more on you than you can bear.* As I woke up, I was repeating that statement over and over.

The more I said it, the more the revelation grew stronger in my spirit. I said to "Man," (my husband's nickname), "I know I'm supposed to go to Pennsylvania and be with my dad and Mom."

John understood the situation and knowing how far I was away from home said, "Okay, I'll check out the plane ticket and the time the plane will leave. I want you to talk with your principal today."

I said, "Okay."

John called the school, and asked me did I talk with the principal yet.

I told him, yes, and I had done all of my lesson plans so that the students would have their work and I could have the time I needed to see about my mother for at least a week.

He said, "Okay, that's good and I have the information for your flight. You can leave this afternoon."

I realized that everything had already been done and all I had to do was to pack my clothes and walk in God's ordained plan. I could feel a knot of fear developing in my stomach and I got real nervous. It had been twenty years since my first and only time flying in an airplane. So I began quoting the Scripture found in II Timothy 1:7 (KJV): "God has not given us the spirit of fear but of power, love and a sound mind." Before I knew it, the red-clay hills of Georgia were behind me and the Allegheny Mountains were before me. It was nice to be home.

My mother stayed in the hospital the whole week that I was there. I asked the nurse how my mother was really doing. The nurse said, "She wasn't eating much." I understood why when I saw the tray of food they brought her. It had a plate of food covered with a warming tray, a bowl of fruit covered with plastic wrap, her juice had a lid, and the silverware was rolled inside a napkin and taped closed. It required a lot of energy to uncover everything so that she could eat. It was next to impossible for her to get to her food on her own because she was weak and had little or no energy.

Mom was a spirit filled beautiful and foxy woman. She was always vibrant, smiling, and usually had something cooking in the kitchen. Now she laid there still, weak and no energy. She had another stroke, irregular heartbeat, plus she was diabetic. It could be controlled but we all knew there was no cure. Along with this, my mother could not walk because of the recent stroke she had had. With tender loving care, I fed my mother and nurtured her as if she were a baby. "Good job," I said to her, "now let's try some vegetables, very good." "Now let's wash it down by drinking some of this juice." I never felt so honored and close to my mother as I did then. She needed me to give back to her the same love she had given to me when I was a baby. Our roles had changed. The doctor told my dad that my mother could go home on that Friday morning. Instructions were given and prescriptions were written for her follow-up care upon release.

My dad quietly said, "You know your mom won't be able to walk upstairs to go to bed or be able to walk to the bathroom."

Trying to be optimistic I said, "I know daddy. We can get a hospital bed to put in the living room and turn it into her bedroom.

My daddy half-heartedly said "okay," in a quiet voice.

My dad and I quickly left the hospital to prepare for my mother's return home from the hospital. In route to having mom's prescription filled, I saw a minister which the family loved and respected. He was very concerned and asked how my mother was doing.

I explained that she was getting released that day and shared with him the plans for her accommodation at home. Sadly I was reminded of a couple of facts: one, I would be returning back to Georgia. And the other thing I was concerned about was that my sister would be faced with the responsibility of caring for our mother and she was already under some stress. She would also be faced with the additional job of hospitality, because of the many visitors that would be coming to the house. My dad was an active deacon at the church and knew a lot of people therefore people would be constantly in and out of our house. That would surely be a burden on my sister and I didn't want that.

I felt a tear slowly roll down one cheek and then another one came rolling down the other cheek but a little faster as the pain of reality began to sink in. My chest felt real heavy like I had just been hit with a brick and my mind got a little fuzzy.

*Suddenly the idea of bringing mom home looked real dim. I hoped the minister was not suggesting that we shouldn't take mom home. How absurd? It was hard to comprehend going home without mom. "Lord, I need Your strength;" I wondered if this was the hidden reason why I had to come home.*

"What do you suggest?" I asked trying to compose my voice and dreading what his answer might be at the same time.

"I know it may hurt, but I....I suggest... a nursing home," he said.

"You think we should put mom in a nursing home?" I asked in disbelief. *I didn't expect this day to come in my mom's life. After all mom wasn't old. I though only 'old people' went to nursing homes.* The minister suggested that I talk with my dad and our pastor before making any decision.

After discussing the situation with my dad and our pastor, we made the painful decision to put mom in a nursing home temporally. I never saw my daddy cry until then.

"Daddy, it's going to be alright, God won't put more on you than you can bear."

He nodded his head and said solemnly, "I know."

Within the hour, everything was recalled from the hospital and arrangements were made at a nursing home for mom to have a room. The next day, I returned to my family in Georgia. A month later the public schools were closed for the Christmas Holidays. One evening, I was cleaning up when I heard the Spirit of the Lord speak softly to me saying, "Take the children and go to Johnstown for Christmas." I went to my husband and shared the revelation with him. He made arrangements for the children and me to go roundtrip to Pennsylvania. I was glad the children would have the opportunity to be with their grandmother who wasn't able to get around or to visit them anymore. By the same token, I was also concerned about how the children would handle being around the other patients in the nursing home.

The children never complained and most of our time was spent going back and forth to the nursing home.    The week passed quickly and we returned home to Georgia.

That Thursday night after we returned home, everyone was sleeping. The children and I had to go back to school the next day and my husband had to go back to work. For some reason I couldn't sleep so I went into the kitchen and read the Scriptures from my Bible. I closed my Bible and started praying: "Father God, *In the name of* Jesus," I began to pray when all *of a sudden a deep feeling of sadness came over me and I began to cry. My cries became deeper and deeper.* Being an intercessor prayer warrior, I cried out to the Lord, "Lord have mercy." *I didn't know if someone was about to go through a crisis, was going through a crisis, or had just gotten out of one,* I cried, "Lord, keep them safe in Your care." I quietly got up and I went to bed.

The next morning when I woke up, I had a song in my spirit. After I dropped the children off to school, I went to work. I couldn't remember all the words to the song but a few words kept coming to me, so I began singing those words over and over, *"Be ready when He comes. Be ready when He comes.*

*Nobody knows the day or the hour, be ready when He comes.* All day long, I would sing or hum those words to myself as I walked down the halls from class to class, to pick up a student or a small group of students.

When I got home from work, my husband pulled me close to him and said in a low and loving voice, "I got some bad news,"

Surprised to see him home before me, I said "What?"

After a short pause he said, "We lost mom, she passed early this morning."

Immediately I started thinking, *Lord, we don't have any money. I exhausted the funds when I flew to Pennsylvania in November and then the children and I went back the last week in December.*

"Lores, did you hear me?" John said concerned about my lack of response.

"Yes baby, I heard you. I was just thinking about our finance."

"I don't want you to worry about that; we'll work it out," he said.

"Maybe we can get an emergency or a bereavement loan on Monday morning," I said as we began to walk towards the couch to sit down. John picked up the telephone and began contacting family and friends and sharing the news about mom's death.

Later that evening, a church member stopped by the house to give her condolences and $20.00 towards anything that the family might need to make the burden easier to bear. I graciously took the gift and placed it in an envelope when she left. All I could think to write on the envelope to distinguish it as *a faith envelope* was *Thank You Jesus.*

More people came on Saturday to give encouraging words and offer their condolences.

That night, before I went to sleep, I read the Scripture found in the six chapter of St. Matthew. I particularly paid attention to verse 6, which says:

"But thou, when thou prayest, enter into thy closet, and when thou hast shut thy door, pray to thy Father which is in secret; and thy Father which seeth in secret shall reward thee openly."

So I prayed unto the Lord. After the last group came on Sunday, there was $1000.00 in the envelope. Praise God! We had more than enough. **I am a living witness that God will work things out and give you what you need when you need it.**

### She Is Just Asleep

John was going to meet us in Pennsylvania for mom's funeral because he had just started a new job and couldn't miss the training that was going to be held in Atlanta the next day. Mysteriously one of the company's trucks was in an accident. Miraculously no one was injured and the training was canceled. Praise God! I would have understood if he had to be at the training, but the Lord knew that I needed my husband with me at that time.

It is a fact that no one wants to lose a mother or a father, however, the lost of my mother was buffered by the comfort in the revelation that was given to me when I read St. John chapter 14:1-6. In these Scriptures, Jesus is comforting His disciples telling them not to be troubled because He was personally going ahead to make preparations ensuring that everything would be in place. This same concept is seen when a mother-to-be hastily prepares everything before the arrival of her newborn baby.

The baby has no knowledge about this world until it comes through the birthing canal. However, when the baby arrives, everything the baby needs is in place. Until the proclaimed day of the Lord comes, I believe the grave acts as a birthing canal for those who die in Christ. The Scriptural bases for this can be found in I Thessalonians 4:13-18 (KJV) and in I Corinthians 15:51-55 (KJV).

A natural example to this revelation was shown to me the first time I stopped to shop at one of the malls in another city, along with a couple of friends, Sophia and Tonya. This was a big mall that had a variety of stores in which to shop. We were hoping to find a lot of bargains. Part of the enjoyment of traveling to this mall was choosing something to eat from the wide selection of vendors. I told my friends that I would catch up with them after I finished eating. When I finished eating I went up the escalator to join them in the store where they said they would be. I looked at the directory and walked all around the second floor trying to find them. Disturbed and flabbergasted, I called one of my friends on my cell phone. I said, "I'm not trying to be funny, but where are you? I don't want you all to think that I have been eating all this time. I've walked all over the second floor and I couldn't find the store you are in."

"Ha ha ha, girl, you're so crazy! Where are you?"said Sophia.

"I'm in front of the jewelry store."

"Go in the clothing store next to it and I'll meet you."

Reluctantly, I walked into the clothing store and when I was halfway through the store, I saw Sophia looking at some items that had been marked down. She looked up when she saw me and started laughing."I'm glad I wore some flat shoes," was all I could say. We continued walking through the store. When we got to the back of the store, it led into another opened area that had approximately twenty additional stores. *Wow, I thought. The revelation came back to me concerning the birthing canal and the grave. If I had not gone through this store, I would not have been able to enter into this area.* Two hours later, we were so tired so, we finally left for home.

When I shared this experience with someone else at a later time, they said they were not aware of the other area that I had spoken about. Some people may say or think, *"What I don't know won't hurt me."* While that statement has some truth to it, from a serious and spiritual perspective the Scripture in Hosea 4:6 (KJV) says: "My people are destroyed for lack of knowledge..."

### The Other Side of Through

A female minister named Annie Doris Spurlin now deceased and also referred to as the 'Daughter of the house,' preached a sermon at our church entitled, "The Other Side of Through." My soul needed to hear that sermon. I never thought about the other side of going through. We only hear of people saying that they are going through something. As I look back over the course of several years of my life, I noticed that so much has happened to me and it was happening at such a rapid rate of speed it made me wonder how I made it over.

For instance, I'm reminded of the closing of two of the schools where I used to work as a counselor which were damaged in the flood of '94. Two new schools were being built and everyone, including the children, were assigned or placed in another school or in a new position. No one wanted to leave their school. It was like the captain who refused to abandon his sinking ship. Nevertheless, everyone had to go. During this period I also experienced the lost of several uncles, aunts, first cousins and friends of whom I had gotten attached to. While all of this was happening, my mind was being pulled and stretched from the graduate courses that I was taking. It felt as though someone was holding each of my arms firmly and was slowly pulling me in opposite directions. My mind, on the other hand, was being broadened. Ideas were challenging and my way of thinking was being expanded.

My faith was really challenged and stretched in 2004. Several events happened that seemed to have had a domino effect in my life and spirit.
- First I was taking the last prerequisite class that I needed to take before I could begin my dissertation
- Secondly my husband decided that he wanted to become a deacon at the church
- Thirdly I lost another first cousin (Michael Hart) that introduced me to my husband thirty-two years ago

- Fourthly I had a second car accident and miraculously remained conscious through it all
- Fifthly my husband was diagnosed with renal (kidney) failure

## The Second Car Accident

Shortly after the school year began several educators had to attend a training session that demonstrated the different assessment tests and how each test was to be given to the students on each grade level. After the workshop was over, I left to go home. It lasted all day long. I drove up to the stop sign from a side street and stopped. After looking both ways, I proceeded to turn left onto the next street. As soon as I made the left turn, a car seemed to come out of nowhere. It was coming straight toward me. *"Where did that car come from?" I didn't see a car anywhere when I pulled out. The car seemed to be coming really fast and it was not slowing down. All I could think of was the Scripture that said, "If you call upon the name of Jesus, He shall save you."* I opened my mouth and called on Him as loudly as I could, "Jesus!"

As soon as I said, "Jesus," the other car hit me on the driver's side. My car started spinning around like a top. I'm sure all of this happened very quickly, but it seemed like my car was spinning around in slow motion like you would go on a merry-go-round. As long as the car kept spinning, I kept saying, "Jesus, Jesus, Jesus." All of a sudden, my car stopped and I felt the seatbelt pull tightly across my shoulder and the airbag hit me in my face. It seemed like time just stood still and everything was frozen in time. After I collected my thoughts about what had just happened I realized that I had just gotten hit by another car. I slowly lifted my head and looked to my side and I noticed that there was smoke in the car. *"I've got to get out of here!" I didn't know if the car was going to blow-up or not.* I tried to open the door but it wouldn't budge. Then I remembered my seatbelt and unhooked it.

"Are you okay?" I heard a lady asking. When I looked out my window, two young ladies, who appeared to be in their twenties, looked at me curiously.

*I thank God that the air conditioning had stopped work-ing in the car so I had rolled the window down to let in some air.*

"Yes, I think so, but I can't open the door."

The door was jammed on the driver's side because of the way the accident had happened. "Can you get out on the passenger's side?" one of the ladies asked.

I told her I thought I could.

I crawled to the other side of the car as fast as I could and the two ladies helped me out of the car and led me across the street and helped me to sit down on the side of a small hill beside the sidewalk.

"My glasses, I don't know what happened to my glasses?" One of the ladies walked back towards the car while the other one called the police to report the accident.

"May I use your cell phone to call my husband?" "Sure," she said as she handed me the phone.

I called my husband and told him that I had just had an accident and that I was okay. I also said that I was going to go to the hospital in the ambulance to get checked out just in case. "Where are you now?" He asked.

I told him the name of the street where I was. "Okay baby, the ambulance will get to where you are before I do. I'll meet you at the hospital and we should get there about the same time. I love you."

"I love you too," I said and returned the phone to the lady.

"Here are you glasses," the other lady said as she handed me the glasses.

"Thank you, where were they?"

"I found your glasses on the other side of the fence on the ground." They were about two feet from where the accident occurred. I was so glad they were not broken.

Carla, my co-worker, who had also attended the workshop, asked me if I was okay and stood next to me.She also called and told the administrators at the school about the accident. When the ambulance came one of the men asked me if I was okay and could I walk. I told him I was okay and I could walk. He helped me get up and walked me to the ambulance and sat me on the side seat in the back of the ambulance. My eyes began to swell up and tears were rolling down my cheeks. I closed my eyes and thanked God. *"Thank You God! Thank You God!" was all my soul could say. "I could have been dead. Lord, You let me witness this accident without going into unconsciousness. You protected me and none of my bones were broken." "Thank You."*

My thoughts of praise and thanksgiving were broken as I heard faint sniffles that grew louder and louder. As I opened my eyes, I noticed that there was another person in the back of the ambulance with me. She was a teenager and looked as though she was around fifteen or sixteen.

"It's okay." I said, trying to console her. If the accident was overwhelming for me as an adult, I could only imagine what she must have been going through. I told her that both of us could have been hurt really bad or even killed, but thank God we were okay. It's going to be okay, I told her.

She nodded her head as her sniffles came under control and got quieter.

After getting checked at the hospital, John took me home and I rested. I had a bruise on my shoulder and chest from the seat belt and my lip was bruised from the air bag when it opened. I know the air bag works and it saved me from having worse injuries. When John and I went to the savage yard to get my valuables from our wrecked car, I was again thankful because the car that hit me just missed hitting the gas tank by about six to eight inches. This stood out to me because I had just filled the gas tank up the day before.

**The Dark Hole**

A follow-up visit from the accidentwas scheduled the next week with another doctor. I went home early from school that day because John wanted to go with me to my doctor's visit. Before we could leave the house the telephone rang. After John answered the telephone, his face went blank.

"What's wrong," I asked.
"The doctor said he wanted to see me today."
"Did he say why?" I said as I moved closer to him.

"No," John said slowly. I told him that as soon as I brought you from your follow-up visit, we would come by his office." "Lord, *please protect my husband,*" was my immediate response. *I'm glad that John made an appointment with the family doctor, which he had been putting off for a long time. He was starting to have regular nose bleeds and some of them were starting to be quite lengthy.*

My follow-up visit didn't last very long and all was well. When we went to the family doctor we were informed that John had high blood pressure and renal (kidney) failure. He wanted John to check into the hospital immediately. The doctor explained that he didn't want us to take this lightly and stated that John appeared to be healthy but he could easily have had a stroke or an aneurism in his sleep. We left to go home and packed an overnight bag for the hospital. Once John was checked into the hospital and placed into a room, life as we knew it was never the same. Our pastor's wife stopped in to visit and brought John some fried chicken to eat.

"I hope you enjoyed that chicken because that will be your last supper for a while," replied a male nurse who came on duty for the night shift. John was not happy with that statement. That nurse turned out to be his "angel in disguise" mainly because John was scheduled to have surgery the next day and the previous nurse, who had just gone off duty, had put the IV needle in the wrong arm. Thank God this was caught immediately and straightened out before any problems could be caused.

That night after I got home with the children I put them to bed so they could get some rest and needed sleep for the next school day. I went into my bedroom (prayer closet) and shut the door. I knelt down on my knees, turned my face to the wall and cried and prayed unto the Lord like Hezekiah did in the 38th chapter of Isaiah.

The surgery went well. John returned home from the hospital and he was in high spirits. That was great because he had gone through a lot. He didn't have time to think about any choices or second opinions that he could make. When his eyes locked into mine I wanted him to know that all was well and I did not want him to worry about anything. I didn't realize it at the time, but my body had shut down on me and I wouldn't be able to do any more assignments for my graduate studies.

It felt as if I had fallen into a deep hole and couldn't find my way out again. The scary part was nobody knew that I had fallen so how could they help me. I would sit at the computer and nothing would happen. I really got alarmed when I got an email from my dissertation chairperson, expressing concern because I had only turned in three of the twelve assignments that were due by the end of the quarter. She reminded me that if all of the work was not submitted before the end of the quarter I would have to retake the class and choose a different topic. That would have meant that all of the research that I had done would have counted for nothing and been totally in vain. The bad news was the quarter was scheduled to end in a month.

Working on my doctorate just didn't seem important anymore and I wanted to quit. In all of my life, I had never been a quitter. I believed in the slogan, "Quitters never win and winners never quit." Somehow I had lost my joy, my praise, and all I wanted to do was sleep after I had taken care of the children. That night when everyone went to sleep, I prayed:

"Lord, I need You. I can't do this by myself. I thank You for everything that You have already done for me. You delivered me from my car accident and from the flood of '94; just as You did David in I Samuel 17:34-36 when You gave him the strength against a lion and a bear. Give me the strength that I need dear Lord.

Show me what to do and how to do it. I need You to do it for me Lord. I need a miracle. In Jesus' name I pray, amen."

When I finished praying, I opened my Bible and read Philippians chapter 4. At that moment peace was restored and I felt my strength returning to me;    especially after I had read Philippians 4:13; which says, "I can do all things through Christ which strengtheneth me." I knew that everything was going to be alright. For the next three weeks, in addition to my job, I was able to complete two class assignments during the week and one assignment on the weekend. Sometimes I had to stay up all night, take a shower and then go to work the next morning. Nevertheless, all of my assignments were submitted and approved by the last week of the quarter. I thanked God for moving on my behalf.

Going through almost anything is hard for all of us, especially when you look at the events, the circumstances, and the timing; to name a few things that deepens the pain. There are many sayings that we say to ourselves to soften the blow such as: "When one door closes, another one opens." "The darkest hour is just before the dawn," and I can't omit the famous saying of, "Joy cometh in the morning." However, no one ever tells us how long the night will last.

You may be going through difficult or different situations worse than anything that I have talked about here. **But I am a living witness that if you trust in the Lord, you will get through it.** The key word is *through*. Psalms 23:4 reminds me that as I walk through any situation I don't have to be afraid. I can walk through with courage as long as I don't stop and get stuck or refuse to go forward. Psalms 34:19 (KJV) encourages us with these words:

"Many are the afflictions of the righteous, but the Lord delivereth him out of them all."

## Guiding Principles/Supportive Scriptures

- When thou passest through the waters, I will be with thee; and through the rivers, they shall not overflow thee: when thou walkest through the fire, thou shall not be burned; neither shall the flame kindle upon thee. Isaiah 43: 2 (KJV)

- I have come to know God as Jehovah-Jireh; my Provider. The Lord will Provide.[22]

- For the Lord will help me; therefore shall I not be confounded: therefore have I set my face like a flint, and I know that I shall not be ashamed. Isaiah 50:7 (KJV)

- Behold, the Lord's hand is not shortened that it cannot save; neither His ear heavy, that it cannot hear. Isaiah 59:1 (KJV)

- ...When the enemy shall come in like a flood, the Spirit of the Lord shall lift up a standard against him. Isaiah 59:19 (KJV)

- And it shall come to pass, that before they call, I will answer; and while they are yet speaking, I will hear. Isaiah 65:24 (KJV)

- But thou, when thou prayest, enter into thy closet, and when thou hast shut the door, pray to thy Father which is in secret; and thy Father which seeth in secret shall reward thee openly. Matthew 6:6 (KJV)

- Many are the afflictions of the righteous; but the Lord delivereth him out of them all. Psalm 34:19 (KJV)

- I can do all things through Christ which strengtheneth me. Philippians 4:13 (KJV)

**Let Us Pray:**

Father, in the Mighty name of Jesus,   I pray that You will forgive me for all of my sins and short comings. I thank You for everything that You have brought me through. I pray for others that You will strengthen those who have come out of a crisis, who are in the middle of a crisis, or who are about to go into one. Remove any bitterness, envy, or unforgiveness that they may have in their heart toward anyone and may peace be restored into their lives. In Jesus' name I pray, amen.

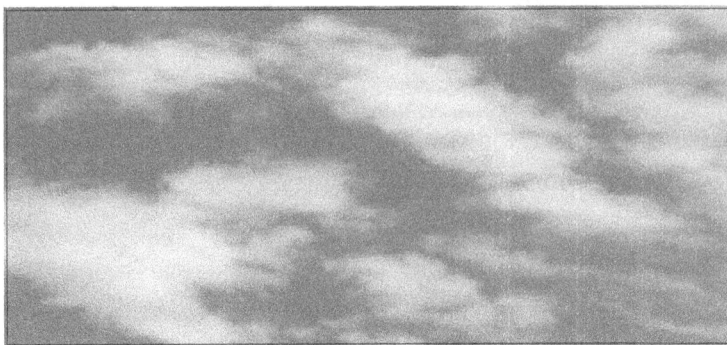

## Chapter Eight

*Behold, I send an Angel before thee,*
*to keep thee in the way, and to bring thee*
*into the place which I have prepared.*
Exodus 23:20 (KJV)

# A New Beginning

I heard a sermon by Bishop T. D. Jakes where he said, "In the critical moments in your life, watch out for the turns." [23] He goes on to say, "Women always lose men in the turns; not in the straight open highways. Nobody trains you or tells you how to take the turn together." So it is with a marriage or with life; many of us "fall-off," because we don't lean with the "curves" that we encounter in life. As we face different trials and tribulations, we have to be willing to make the necessary changes that are needed to keep on living

### I Want To Live

I will never forget the profound words that John spoke to me when he was in the hospital; "Baby, I want to live."

I thanked God that John had that attitude. This reminded me of the saying, "Our attitude determines our altitude." Once again, we were reminded of the words spoken by Jesus, found in John 11:4 which says:

"This sickness is not unto death, but for the glory of God, that the Son of God might be glorified thereby." Moreover, Psalm 118:17 declares, "I shall not die but live, and declare the works of the Lord."

Since that day, it seems like that is what John has been doing, declaring that he will not die but live. Tears filled my eyes as I watched and witnessed the ordination service when John was ordained to become a deacon of the church. I thought to myself, *is this the same man that felt like I prayed all the time, went to church too much, wasn't happy with me paying tithes, or got a little irritated when I was diligent with teaching the children at Sunday School and at Bible study? I can remember when John would get embarrassed when I stood up to praise God.*

Truly, God works in mysterious ways. The Lord did a Saul to Paul conversion, like the one found in Act chapter nine, right in front of my eyes. Indeed, John was a chosen vessel. The same boldness, courage, and love that John has for people was now being used to bring glory to God's name.

Now John gets to the church before I do, and many times he will beat me standing up to praise God. He is the Superintendent of the Sunday School, and teaches Sunday School and Bible study faithfully and with eloquence. My heart is delighted and I am so thankful and honored for all that the Lord has done to and through my husband.

John loves fishing and would go all of the time. He still goes fishing but now, he also is a "fisher of men." **I'm a living witness that prayer changes things. If we give the situation to the Lord, He will work it out.**

## He Will Work It Out

Whatever the situation, I know that God will work it out. Even when you can't hear His voice or it seems like all hope is gone; God will work it out. John had to stop working because of his health. Two years passed before he was able to get his disability income. Thank God, the Lord kept us and we made it. David knew that God would work it out. He put his trust in the Lord as can be seen in the Psalm which says: "I have been young, and now am old; yet have I not seen the righteous forsaken, nor his seed begging bread," Psalms 37:25 (KJV).

That is because of His divine care. The Scriptures speak of how the fowls of the air are fed and how the lilies grow. Likewise, we are encouraged with these words in Matthew 6:33 (KJV), "But seek ye first the kingdom of God, and His righteousness; and all these things shall be added unto you." Through all of the experiences that you may have, I think Paul covers the issue of "being in want" well in Philippians 4:11-12 (KJV). It says:

"…For I have learned, in whatsoever state I am, therewith to be content. I know both how to be abased, and I know how to abound; every where and in all things I am instructed both to be full and to be hungry, both to abound and to suffer need."

When you know that nobody but the Lord brought you through 'this or that situation,' then you will be able to give God a testimony and the next time you have to go through a similar situation you will be able to say these words with boldness:

"Let your conversation be without covetousness; and be content with such things as ye have; for He hath said, I will never leave you, nor forsaken you. So I can boldly say, The Lord is my helper, and I will not fear, what man shall do." Hebrew 13:5-6 (KJV)

When I was growing up, my friend's grandmother stayed with her family before she died. Whenever anyone would say anything to her, she would always say "You ought to talk that you know and testify what you see." I thought that saying was so funny, especially the way that she said it, and it always stayed with me. When I grew older, I was astonished when I found this similar statement in John 3:11 (KJV) which says, "Verily, verily I say unto thee, we speak that we do know, and testify that we have seen." Over the years, I can say that I have seen with my own eyes how the Lord will work things out; if we let Him. I will share a few of these examples with you such as your health, your marriage, and your dreams.

**Your Health**

John has his good days and he has his bad days. However, his good days outweigh his bad days and as the song says, "God has been so good to me, I won't complain." Third John 2 (KJV) says:

"Beloved, I wish above all things that thou mayest prosper and be in health, even as thy soul prospereth."

We know that this is God's desire for us. This statement is supported in II Peter 1:20-21 (KJV). It says: "Knowing this first that no prophecy of the Scripture is of any private interpretation. For the prophecy came not in old time by the will of man: but holy men of God spake as they were moved by the Holy Ghost." Moreover, this same passage in the NLT (New Living Translation) says it this way: "Above all you must understand that no prophecy in Scripture ever came from the prophets themselves, or because they wanted to prophesy. It was the Holy Spirit who moved the prophets to speak from God. II Peter 1:20-21(NLT).

It's good to know that well wishes are sent our way. A familiar saying that you may have heard is, "We are a product of what we eat." If we believe that this statement is true, then we will strive to put healthy food into our bodies. This principle is also the same with putting healthy thoughts into our minds. Paul encourages us with these words:

"Finally brethren, whatsoever things are true, whatsoever things are honest, whatsoever things are just, whatsoever things are pure, whatsoever things are lovely, whatsoever things are of good report; if there be any virtue, and if there be any praise, think on these things." Philippians 4:8 (KJV)

When we do this, it is written:

"And the peace of God, which passeth all understanding, shall keep your hearts and minds through Christ Jesus." Philippians 4:7 (KJV)

"Thou will keep him in perfect peace, whose mind is stayed on Thee; because he trusteth in Thee." Isaiah 26:3 (KJV)

**I am a living witness that the Lord will keep you in perfect peace, if you trust His Word and keep your mind on Him.**

## Marriage

When your heart is at peace, then it is easier to fall in love. Eventually the feelings that we have for another person may lead to marriage, especially if the feelings are mutual and both parties are available. Falling in love is easy; it's the staying together that is hard. The act of "giving," from both parties, is a large part of being married. The range of giving could range from something as common as money and affection to things that are abstract such as patience and forgiveness.

Dr. Dorothy Tennov, a professor of psychology, has done long–range studies on the in-love phenomenon (and later published a book called Love and Limerence). After studying 500 people of different backgrounds and age groups, she concluded that the average life-span of a romantic obsession is between six months and two years.[24] After John and I decided to stay committed to our vows and save the marriage, we searched for more active things that we could do together as a couple. We found the answer to this in "The Couple's Ministry," a group founded by our previous pastor Rev. Jimmy Ewing, whom we love and respect deeply.

The group was open to anyone, although presently, it consisted of four to five regular couples. Since it was a small group, we alternated our meetings by going to each other's homes once a month. The evening usually consisted of sharing, laughter and refreshments and/or desserts. The meetings had no set agenda except for having discussions on an assigned chapter in a book on marriage that we were reading (not on anyone's personal marriage). In one of our meetings, Rev. Ewing made the following comment during the discussion, he said,

"When we take our vows, we are saying "I do" to the good, to the bad, to sickness and in good health...until death do us part." No matter how good the good gets or how bad the bad gets.

On the Day of Judgment, God is going to ask you why you didn't keep your part of the "I do" in your marriage. God is not going to want to hear you say, "But you don't know what he or she did or said to me." (Personal Communication, July 12, 2008).

During the class we were having discussions and home-work assignments from a book called *The Five Love Languages* by Gary Chapman. The book explains how each of us has a primary (main) and a secondary love language that we speak. After thirty years of marriage counseling Mr. Chapman (2004) concluded, that there are five emotional love languages; although there may be different dialects (variations).[25] If you and your spouse have a different love language, then it will be hard to understand how to love each other. According to Chapman, we must be willing to learn our spouse's primary love language, as well as our own, if we are to become effective communicators of love. They are:

- Words of Affirmation
- Quality time
- Receiving gifts
- Acts of Service
- Physical Touch

The Apostle Paul addressed the importance of love in Colossians 3:14 (KJV). It states that love binds everything together in perfect harmony (NLT) I Peter 4:8 (KJV) declares, "Above all things, we are to have fervent charity among ourselves; for charity shall cover the multitude of sins." The word charity is often used in parallel with the word love. This correlation can be seen in I Corinthians 13:13 (KJV), which states: "And now abideth faith, hope, charity (love), these three; but the greatest of these is charity."

Because love and affection are so important in a marriage, every year, we made reservations at a restaurant to eat dinner as a group for Valentine's Day. We also went on a honeymoon retreat at Jekyll Island. The only time that we were to be with the other couples during the retreat was for dinner, usually on the first night. After that, we were to take advantage of not being around any children, family members, work, or the telephone so we could enjoy our spouses and open our imaginations to dream.

**Your Dreams**

God has planted in us dreams, ideas, passions, imagination, creativity, and hope. These things require the right environment in order to flourish and come to fruition (The Glory of Living, p. 75). [26]

We can listen to the words of Solomon in Ecclesiastes to gain wisdom concerning our dreams. He says, "To everything there is a season, and a time to every purpose under the heaven (Ecclesiastes 3:1, KJV)."

This helps us to know that it is okay for us to dream. However, we have to have a dream and believe that God can do it. The Lord will do His part and we, on the other hand, have to do our parts (Rev. Solomon Loud, July, 2006). It is hard to know the path (Career-wise or Spiritual) that we are to take. That is why it is important to pray and listen for direction from God. Proverbs 3:5-6 (KJV) say:

"Trust in the Lord with all thine heart;
and lean not unto thine own understanding.
In all thy ways acknowledge Him,
and He shall direct thy paths."

Furthermore, these words are written in Ecclesiastes 5:3 (KJV): "For a dream cometh through the multitude of business." This implies that we can't just sit around and expect our dream to just fall into our laps. You have to be willing to work for it in order to see it happen. This reminds me of another saying, "Anything worth having is worth working for." According to Webster (1984), business can mean: work, calling, employment, job line, occupation, and the pursuit of it.[27] It you are going to work toward a dream that means that you have to get a higher education after completing high school, such as Vocational training, technical or Community College, or a 4 year college. Dress for success according to the profession that you have chosen. Speak appropriately, communicate with others, learn work ethics, be respectable, and work as a team player.

Even when you do all of this, your dream still may not happen, or come in the time-frame that you wanted it to happen. Sometimes, I get the things that I pray for; other times I do not. However, that doesn't mean that God isn't God or that He can't do what He says He can do. Remember, delayed doesn't mean denied. I have found that the answers to my prayers are either yes, no, or not now. Nevertheless, whatever my answer is, I am confident     that the decision is in my best interest.

If the answer is "Yes", then that means that the Lord has equipped me with everything (resources) I need to be successful. If the answer is "No", then I know the choice is not for me. If the answer is "Not now", then that means that I am not ready yet. The key word is "Yet" and it implies that He is getting me ready or will get me ready in due season. If I insist and try to go out before the Lord prematurely, I can have a lot of regrets, remorse, or heartaches or even failure that could have been avoided.

The prophet Isaiah assures us that the Lord knows what's best for us when he says,
"For My thoughts are not your thoughts, neither are you ways My ways, saith the Lord.
 For as the heavens are higher than the earth, so are My ways higher than your ways and
My thoughts than your thoughts." (Isaiah 55:8-9, KJV)

It is important that we understand that it is not the Lord's will to hurt us or to see us hurt. If we really believe that the Lord directs our paths then we can trust what was written by the prophet Jeremiah when he wrote this passage in the Scripture,

"For I know the thoughts that I think toward you, said the Lord, thoughts of peace, and not of evil, to give you an expected end." Jeremiah 29:11 (KJV)

Further assurance is given to us by Paul; when he wrote:

"Eyes have not seen, nor ears heard, neither have it entered in the heart of man, the things which God has prepared for them that love Him." I Corinthians 2:9

## A Prepared Place

Giving honor to God, I obtained a doctorate's degree in January of 2006. To my surprise, twelve people (my immediate family, my dad, my aunt Pricilla, Valarie – now Dr. Williams–a fellow doctorial colleague, and cousins from the Reese family Willie Pearl and Dolores) drove five and a half hours to attend my graduation ceremony in Sarasota, Florida. It was raining as we drove to the graduation and when we were several miles from the university, we got a flat tire.

My husband drove the van to the shoulder of the highway. Several people got out to look at the damages or to call AAA. The interstate was busy with cars trying to get to their destinations. My dad placed a handkerchief on the point of his umbrella and waved it in the air. Within several minutes, a car pulled up behind us and a middle aged Caucasian man, who was a Christian, got out of his car and changed the flat tire for us.

The only thing that he would take from us was a thank you. I will always be thankful for this genuine act of kindness. He mentioned that his wife was expecting a baby. I pray that his family will always be blessed.

It was really touching to see my friend Laurie, my colleague from thirty years ago and her husband, Joe, who flew in from New Jersey. Seven additional cousins drove from various parts of Florida to attend my graduation. Laurie made reservations for a party of twenty-one people to eat at a restaurant that was designed with large picture windows that overlooked the ocean. The speaker from the graduation, was seated at the table next to ours; along with other dignitaries from the university. Words can't explain how elated and thankful I felt to obtain this degree and to receive the support from my family and friends. No one hesitated or complained about making the trip for the graduation.

A few months after I graduated, I heard the faint words "Its time to move," in a small still voice. I was so taken a-back that I turned around to see who was behind me, but I saw no one. After a few seconds, I heard the words again, "It's time to move." Immediately, I thought of Samuel, when the Lord called him and he kept getting up going to see what Eli the Priest wanted, only to discover that no one had called him. After Samuel had done this for the third time, he was instructed to say, "Speak Lord for Thy servant heareth Thee." Therefore I said to myself, move?" Then I asked, "What do you mean move?" Needless to say, I got no answer.

I prayed and asked the Lord, "Lord, how can I ask my husband for this huge request at this time in our lives?" We had accumulated nine years worth of furniture and assets. I heard the words in my spirit; "*I'll show you how to do it.*" About a week later, I asked the Lord to show me where I was supposed to move. One night I had a dream that I was inside of a house. There was fog all around me and slowly the fog lifted, and I was able to see my face. I looked to my left and to my right and then I looked in front of me and covered my mouth in surprise and awe. As I covered my mouth, I said these words, "It's so beautiful!" Immediately after that everything vanished. After that I woke up. That morning, as I got ready for work, I said to the Lord, "Is this all I have to go on? How are we supposed to find the house with this small amount of information? The house could be anywhere!"

Later that day John said, "Baby if we start looking for a house you know the realtor is going to try and get you to buy a house right now."

"Baby, I know that's true; I also believe that the house the Lord wants to bless us with will be gone if we don't look now. I believe that's why He said it's time to move."

"I don't know if I'm up to packing up our house," my husband said reluctantly.

"The Lord will show us what to do and how to do it. I just needed your permission," I said excitedly.

After a long pause, John said, "Okay."

John got the boxes and I started packing the small things that we weren't using in each room, and then moved to the decorations on the wall.

John got with his cousin Mattie, a realtor and she gave us a list of houses that were for sale that were located on the south, east, west, and north sides of town. The houses also had the items that we were looking for. Two or three times a week John and I would go down the list and look inside of the houses to see if we liked it. Sometimes my Aunt Pricilla would go with me if John didn't feel like going. Finally, John and I narrowed the choices down to two and then to one house. We told Mattie that we had decided on a particular house. Then my cousin asked the "Million Dollar question."

"Lores, did you say that it was beautiful?"

I had forgotten that I shared the testimony of the vision of the house with her and I tried to remember that first word that I said the first time that I saw the house. I remembered! *I said "the house was nice." Yes, I said that "this is really nice."*

"No, I didn't say that this was beautiful. I said that this was really nice. I'm sorry, this is not the house."

I looked pleadingly at my husband and said, "We can't sign. This isn't the house."

He said, "Okay, I hope we can find it."

Mattie, who was also a Christian said, "Okay, we'll keep looking until we find it."

The next week, John and I were at a low peak with the search for the house. We called Mattie and asked her if we could see the inside of a certain house.

"Okay." She said, "It's preferable that we show at least two houses on an outing."

We agreed on a day and time that she would pick us up. When Mattie picked us up to view the houses, she suggested that we look at a certain house first and end up looking at the one we wanted to see last, since we had viewed part of it already. We agreed and went to look at the first house. When we got to the house, the owner opened the door and was holding a small dog that was almost identical to the dog we owned.

"Hello, you all just come on in and feel free to look around.

"Hello" we said as we went inside. We walked through the house and outside in the backyard. When I came back inside, I went in the foyer and stood still. I looked to my left and saw a glass door. I looked to my right and saw another glass door. Then I looked right in front of me and looked into a mirror on the wall. As I covered my mouth, I quietly whispered the words, "It's so beautiful."

"What do you think; is this the one?" asked Mattie.
"Yes" I said, "This is the one!"
I turned to John and asked, "Do you like it Baby?" He said, "Yes." We said our goodbyes and left to go view the second house.

We arrived at the second house and went through each room observing them carefully. The house had a gothic design and had a swimming pool with a changing area built on the deck. The inside of the house had a large living room and master bedroom as well as other features that were nice. However, my excitement had changed because my heart was already sold on the previous house. When we returned home we did the paperwork to make a bid for the first of the two houses we had looked at. Our realtor informed us that another realtor also made a bid the same day on the same house for her client. Needless-to-say, we got the bid.

I can't believe that after all of this; the bank refused to sign the "Lender's Agreement" form agreeing to be the lender; even though we had the required amount of money needed for the down payment for the house in the bank.

"Mom does this mean that we are not going to move and need to put everything back?" my daughter asked.

I'm reminded of a quote that says, "Without faith nothing is possible, with it, nothing is impossible (Bethune, 2009)."[28] I said, "We're going to move baby; we're going to move by faith" I said with a new determination and continued packing.

The next bank we tried said yes. The Lord blessed us to be the new owners. I believe that it is important for anyone who is walking by faith to continue to move forward, in spite of what you may see or what you may hear. **I'm a living witness that there is nothing too hard for God to do.**

### There Is Nothing Too Hard For God

I'm reminded of the familiar expression, **"It's already done!" I think ... Well ... I'm a living witness that this statement is true.** When we moved in, our furniture blended in with the color scheme that was already in each room and it seemed as if we had always lived there. I really felt like we were walking in our destiny. Immediately I began to feel like this was where I was meant to be so that I could finish this book. I believe that sometimes the main thing that stops us from moving forward is fear itself. There were many times when I had to make a decision and I wasn't sure if the right decision was being made. After prayer and meditation all I could do was to trust in God.

In the beginning one of my main concerns was having or keeping enough food in the pantry. David reminds us in Psalms 37:25 with these words; "I have been young and now am old; yet I have not seen the righteous forsaken or his seed begging bread." If I thought that we were getting low on food, someone would invite us for dinner or I would pick up a few items. It seemed like the pantry would always be full.

Moreover, whenever it was time for me to do something that I had never done before, there was always someone close by who was there to teach me how to do it or lead me to someone who could do it. For example, paying someone to cut the hedges and culture the landscape was costly so I put on working gloves and started working at what I knew to do. My neighbor, Mr. Willie, who has a beautiful land-scaped yard, helped me to understand what the different plants were in our yard and how to care for them.    I contacted my friend Cindy, who also has beautiful plants in her yard. She showed me how to care for the flowers that I had before we moved in and she agreed to help me again, only this time, it was on a larger scale.

When I brought Miss Cindy over to the house, she said, "Dolores," speaking in a serious tone, "You're going to need the right equipment to do this type of work. It's easier when you use the right equipment. We can use mine until you get what you need." I said, "Okay Cindy, just show me what I need and I will get it." The more I worked outside doing gardening the more I realized how therapeutic it was. Many days I had a lot of stress inside of me because of the basic pressures from home, the workplace, grad-school, and from the church. It seemed each one was pulling on me at the same time and all in different directions.

However, when I worked in the garden I felt so at peace and any problems that I was dealing with became clear. My hearing would get unclogged and I would remember different truths that I had learned in the past or I would quietly hear a Scripture in my ear.

One Scripture that comes to my mind is the parable of the tares and the wheat (Matthew 13:24-30, NKJ), which tells of a man who planted seeds in his field. But while he slept, his enemy came and planted weeds among the seeds. As the plants grew, weeds also grew among the plants. When the man inquired and asked if he should pull the weeds up, the reply was, no, leave the weeds alone because you might pull up wheat in the process. Let them grow up together until the harvest time and then do the separating.

The overwhelming task of pulling weeds from around various plants is a frustrating task and it was hard for me to do at first because I couldn't tell one from the other. But the more I did it the easier it became and slowly I began to notice the difference. "What a cumbersome task!" I said as I was almost about to pull a plant out of the ground. "What a great camouflage! It appeared that the weeds were trying to hide behind or beside the plant in hopes that it wouldn't be noticed or discovered." It's funny because sometimes as humans we do the same thing. As the plants bloomed into beautiful flowers, I could without hesitation pull the weeds from around them.

It's hard to believe that we have been in our home for four years. As time passed we were able to hire a gardener to care for the flowers. That freed me up so I could turn my attention to the calling that the Lord has on my life.

## He Did It Again

However, I am so thankful that I have flowers around me again. As I remember, years ago, we had a lot of flowers in the house where we lived. At that time, with amazement, I knew that I only had enough energy to focus on nourishing and keeping myself healthy. In fact, sometimes I smile in gratitude as I think back and remember the statement that I made when I was recuperating from my car accident, "Plants, I only have enough energy to nourish and keep either you or me healthy, and I vote for me." Then I slowly started giving my plants away. Now, I am overwhelmed with beautiful flowers around me again.

Just as you have happy memories, there are painful ones as well and as you have sunny days, there will be rainy days as well. It seemed as if a rain cloud came and stood over my house. It was as if God was warning me that a storm was on its way. When I came home from work on Thursday, August 6, 2009, my husband told me that dad had called and said that my brother William, affectionately called Boot, was swelling up and refused to go to the hospital. *It was already my intentions to call him that day because it was his birthday. Also I wanted to see if he had gotten his birthday card from us.* My heart was full and heavy as I said, "What's happened? What's wrong with Boot?

"I don't know," said John, "that is all that your dad told me. He wants you to call him." "Okay," I said.

Immediately, I laid my bags down and picked up the telephone and dialed Boot's telephone number." My sister-in-law, Tiny, answered the phone in a raspy voice, saying, "Hello." "Hey sis," I said, "Daddy called John and told him about Boot's condition."

"That's right Lores, I called the EMS (Emergency Medical Service) and they checked him out and said that his vital signs were okay. However, they encouraged him to go to the hospital to get checked for the swelling, but he refused." "May I speak to him?"

"Sure, she replied, "Boots, your sister is on the phone."

"Hello," he whispered in a faint voice.

"I softly told my brother happy birthday."But Boot mumbled some words that I couldn't understand and after that, I heard him put the phone down.

I decided to let him rest because I could tell that he was weak. *I'll call and check on him tomorrow.* The next day Boot did sound much stronger when I spoke with him. He didn't talk for long, but I could understand everything that he said. "Boot, you need to go to the hospital and let the doctors examine you," I said as lovingly and firmly as a younger sister could say it to a big brother.

"They gave me a clean bill of health." Boot said trying to convince me.

"Boot, nobody gave you a clean bill of health. Please go to the hospital and get checked." Once again, Boot laid the telephone down. My heart was saddened because, this time I knew that he was finished talking to me.

That Saturday, I was over to my aunt Pricilla's house, we laughed and talked and prayed. As we prayed, a deep feeling of sadness came over me and I began to cry. My cries became deeper and I began to say, "Lord have mercy!" Once again, I wasn't sure if someone was about to go through a crisis, was going through a crisis, or had just gotten out of one. As I finished praying, the following words started coming out in a song, "Be ready when He comes, be ready when He comes. Nobody knows the day or the hour, be ready when He comes." After that moment, my auntie and I didn't say much because there wasn't any thing else to say.

When I came home from work on Tuesday, John was teary-eyed. He looked real solemn, and embraced me as he said, "Your dad called and said we lost Boot today." It took a minute for the words to sink in. "Lores, did you hear me? Your dad said Boot died. My mind drifted away to our finances. In order for *John Sr., to take the trip to Pennsylvania, the three of us would need to fly.* I thought to myself, *we just paid for three round trip tickets for my step daughter, our daughter and my self to fly to Chicago, Illinois for our son's Naval graduation from Boot Camp. Also, we paid for our dad and our family reunion expenses that were held last month in July.*

"What happened?" I managed to get out.

"I don't know your dad was upset so I didn't ask him.

I thank God for my husband because I just didn't have the strength to call anyone. I'm so glad that John took on the painful task of calling family members to let them know about our loss. The next few days seemed like a blur, but by Thursday morning plans were made for us to go to Pennsylvania. Along with the emergency finances that we had, our church, and the support from cousin Hakim and Brenda, once again, we had everything that we needed for the trip. **He did it again.** John and I were so grateful.

Every day in Johnstown was filled with close ties, family, and friends. We all reminisced and talked about our childhood days. My brother William (Boot) was the first of my siblings to die. I really felt perplexed. Another link is now missing out of our chain or should I say, in our immediate family. Two out of eight candles have gone out.

I listened to and embraced my family and childhood friends. I was inspired to write the poem entitled *The Man in the*

*Mirror.* During the funeral I read the poem. Since my brother William was a retired veteran, they played Taps at the end of the funeral after which they also did a 21 gun salute. I thought about the words written by King Solomon (Ecclesiastes 3:1) which says, "To everything there is a season, and a time to every purpose under the heaven; A time to be born and a time to die."

**It's Time**

Time seemed to go by so quickly and we returned to Georgia and continued with our day to day schedule. I have always heard the saying that, "When someone dies, someone is born at the same time. One evening after we ate dinner, John and I were talking about our anniversary. We decided to start planning early for our anniversary because next year on February 16, 2010 we will be celebrating our 25th (Silver) Anniversary. I became very quiet and began to reflect on everything that the Lord had brought us through; the problems we had in our marriage and how we both have changed over the years.

After we talked about these different situations, I was shocked when John looked at me real serious and said, "Starting today, can we start courting again?"

"Okay," I said as I looked at my husband and thought, *that's the man I married 24 years ago.* We decided that we would renew our wedding vows.

**I'm a living witness that God can work anything out if you give it to Him. You should confess your faults and forgive others.** With that surprise, I realized that it was also time to give birth. *Yes, I'm going to have a spiritual baby!*

When it is your hour and you are about to deliver or give birth to a baby, you may be delirious. That means, you may say or do things that you would not normally say or do. Everyone acts in different ways. I have seen people scream, stand up and start walking back and forth as they repeated a word or moan. Some women sit and bend over holding their stomachs, some want loved ones near to encourage them, some don't want you to say anything at all, or they may squeeze a love-one's hand to help embrace the pain. This is not a time to worry about how you look or worry about who is looking at you. Your main goal is to birth this baby that has been living and growing inside of you. Sometimes you can tell how sharp or frequent the pains are by the deepness of the cry. If the pain gets to be too much to bear or if you're unable to deliver the baby naturally, the doctor can give you an epidural shot depending on how far along you are in the birthing process. So is it with delivering a spiritual baby; you may jump up and down, take off running or they may shout the highest praise, hallelujah or glory to God. There is no epidural shot, so you have to experience every pain.

It is at that moment that the doctor or nurse will say, PUSH. In the natural realm that means to bear down with everything inside of you and with all of your might, then PUSH until the baby is in position to be birthed. These same letters –PUSH- mean something different when giving birth to a spiritual baby.

Spiritually, male or female may give birth to a spiritual baby. However, the helpers are intercessors and prayer warriors, not doctors and nurses.

Spiritually, the acronym for PUSH means: **Pray Until Something Happens.** You may have to do this several times before the baby is born. Only you and time alone with Jesus can birth your baby. The degree and frequency of the pain may determine the type of baby you are birthing and how close you are to birthing what the Lord has placed inside of you. It has out grown you and needs to come out. Once it's out you can begin helping, teaching, healing, and even perform miracles to bring glory to God's Holy name.

A couple of months ago, I had a dream and I woke up crying because I couldn't deliver the baby I was carrying. I am so glad that I was dreaming, because, it wasn't my time to deliver. But now it is my hour. The time has come for me to deliver and it is indeed, a **New Beginning.**

## Guiding Principles/Supportive Scriptures

- Behold, I send an Angel before thee, to keep thee in the way, and to bring thee into the place which I have prepared. Exodus 23:20 (KJV)

- I came to know God as Jehovah-El-Shaddai; the Almighty God.[29]

- I shall not die, but live, and declare the works of the Lord. Psalms 118:17 (KJV)

- I have been young and now am old; yet have I not seen the righteous forsaken, nor his seed begging bread. Psalms 37:25 (KJV)

- But seek ye first the kingdom of God, and His righteousness; and all these things shall be added unto you. Matthew 6:33 (KJV)

- Beloved, I wish above all things that thou mayest proper and be in health, even as thy soul prospereth. Third John 2 (KJV)

- Thou will keep him in perfect peace, whose mind is stayed on Thee: because he trusteth in Thee. Isaiah 26:3 (KJV)

- To everything there is a season, and a time to every purpose under the heaven. Ecclesiastes 3:1 (KJV)

- For a dream cometh through a multitude of business; and a fool's voice is known by multitude of words. Ecclesiastes 5:3 (KJV)

- But as it is written, Eyes have not seen, nor ears heard, neither has it entered into the heart of man, the things which God hath prepared for them that love Him. I Corinthians 2: 9 (KJV)

**Let Us Pray:**

Father, in the Mighty name of Jesus, I thank You for everything that You have already done. Thank You for what You are doing and will do in my life. Help us to keep our minds on You, then we will have perfect peace. It is Your desire that we should be in good health and prosper. We know that a dream comes from a multitude of effort. According to Your Word, You will perfect that which is lacken in us. It is also written in Psalm 18:28 that You will light my candle and that You have enlighten my darkness. Strengthen those who are going through a transition or a change in their lives. Take away any fears that would prohibit us from having a new beginning. Give us the courage that we need to run this race, in Jesus' name we pray, amen.

# NOTES

## Introduction

[1.] Sapp, M. (2008). Never could have made it without you. (CD). Retrieved From www.youtube. com

[2.] Arnette, K. A. (2004). In, Ever rising: From tragedy and pain to triumph and gain. Goldsboro NC. Spirit Reign Publication.

## Chapter One
## This Is The Day

[3] Teaching portfolio required of newly hired teachers.

[4] Two hospitalized after accident. (1990, January 8). *The Albany Herald*, p. 2A.

[5] Stone, N. (1944). Jehovah-Rohi [11]. March 23, 2008, *Names of god.*

## Chapter Two
## The Prayer Of Faith

[6] Palmyra Medical Center (1990, January 8). History and physical examination (hospital number 111875). Albany, GA.

[7] Palmyra Medical Center (1990, January 8). Nursing progress notes (hospital number 111875). Albany, GA

[8] (2006, May 17). Coma. Retrieved November 11, 2007 from MayoClinic.com

[9] Sumrall, L. (1982). The lord is peace (Jehovah-Shalom). In *The names of god* (pp. 173-182). New Kensington, PA: Whitaker House.

## Chapter Three
## Love Lifted Me

[10] Angels watching over me (2006, May 30). http://www.youtube.com [by virtue].

[11] Sumrall, L. (1982). The lord god most high (Jehovah-Leon). In *The names of god* (pp. 71-81). New Kensington, PA: Whitaker House.

## Chapter Four
## Restoration

[12] Sumrall, L. (1982). The Lord is conqueror (Jehovah-Nissi). In *The names of God* (pp.161-172). New Kensington, pa: Whitaker House.

## Chapter Five
## Faith and the Promise

[13] John 11:14 [KJV].

[14] Sumrall, L. (1982). The lord is healer (Jehovah-Repheka). In *The names of god* (pp.119-131). New Kensington, pa: Whitaker House.

## Chapter Six
## The Two Shall Be One

[15] Hiscox, T. E., (1968). The marriage service, In *The star book for ministers* (pp, 197-211).Valley Forge, PA: The Judson Press.

[16] John 10:9, 3:3. [KJV].

[17] Hiscox, T. E., (1968). The marriage service, In *The star book for ministers* (pp, 197-211).Valley Forge, PA: The

Judson Press.

[18] Sumrall, L. (1982). The lord is there (Jehovah-Shamah). In *The names of god* (pp.183-196). New Kensington, pa: Whitaker House.

## Chapter Seven
## From Trials to Triumphs

[19] Exodus 14: 21-21 [KJV].

[20] Flood watch'94, (July). WALB-TV Channel 10, [video tape].

[21] Kim, S. (1998, September 10). GA spring flood work continues. Retrieved November 8, 2008, http://www.diasternews.net/news/article.php?articied=506

[22] Sumrall, L. (1982). The lord will provide (Jehovah-Jireh). In *The names of god* (pp.103-117). New Kensington, PA: Whitaker House.

## Chapter Eight
## A New Beginning

[23] Jakes, T. D. (2009, April 28). Helping woman understand men [video]. www.Youtube.com.

[24] Marshall, G, A. (2003). That crazy thing called loved. Retrieved May 2, 2009, http://guardian.co..uk/theobserver/2003

[25] Chapman, G. (2004). What happens to love after the wedding. In *The five love languages: How to express heartfelt commitment to your mate* (pp. 10-17). Chicago: Northfield.

[26] Munroe, M., Dr. (2005). The glory of becoming. In *The glory of living* (pp. 65-84). Nassau, Bahamas: Destiny Image.

[27] Webster's II new riverside university dictionary. (1984). Boston, MA: Houghton Mifflin.

[28] Bethune, M. M. Without faith nothing is possible, with it, nothing is impossible. Retrieved May 10 from http://brainy quote.com/quotes//keywords/impossible.htm

[29] Sumrall, L. (1982). The almighty god (Jehovah-EI-Shaddai). In *The names of god* (pp.83-102). New Kensington, PA: Whitaker House.

# Afterword

**John Floyd Sr.** is medically retired. He is also the Superintendent of the Sunday school and a Deacon at the New Beginning Missionary Baptist Church. Thank you for your unconditional love. I love you with all my heart.

**Tonescha Lashawn Sibley**, my beautiful and loving step-daughter, is finishing her classes for Medical Coding Specialist. May God bless you and our grandson Quientel Johnord Cutliff for your unconditional love.

**John Emmanuel Floyd Jr.**, is enlisted in the United States Navy. Your life was spared for a reason. God will reveal the purpose for your life and lead you to your destiny in due season.

**Davina Jonette Floyd**, my beloved daughter is a junior in high school. You are multi-talented. Let God order your steps and you'll bring glory to His Holy name.

**Dolores Floyd, Ed.D** is a Professional School Counselor at one of the elementary schools in Albany, Georgia. She is also on the minister's staff at New Beginning Missionary Baptist Church where she teaches Sunday School and Bible Study to the Youth.

# The Man In The Mirror

### (In Loving Memory of William Henry Hart)

Stop and look at the man in the mirror,
Tell me what do you see?
Is it someone who is scared, sad or angry?
Or have you been set free?

You can only have true freedom,
If you accept Jesus as your savior,
He will give you strength and wisdom,
To help you change any behavior.

Take a long look, at the man in the mirror,
How do you spend your day?
Do you fear God and do what He say?
Or do you only laugh and play.

*Continued*

It's God's desire for everyone to have joy,
and courage for what we must face.
Let's remember that we need Jesus,
to have the strength to run this race.

When you look at the man in the mirror,
I hope you'll see someone humble and true;
A person who has accepted Christ,
Looking back at you.

After you have fought your last battle,
and the battle has been won;
Beloved, you want to hear the Master say,
Servant of God, well done.

By
Dr. Dolores Hart-Floyd
(8-17-09)

# Acknowledgments

I want to thank my first cousin David Mitchell who went to my wrecked vehicle and collected all my valuables from the car. Thanks Mitch!

Thank you Minister Gwen Weston for supervising the ladies at Kingdom Life Christian Center to sing and pray for me around the clock.

LeDeadra Sullivan-Brown, thank you for your prayers, your help with obtaining needed information, and for your constant support.

Rev. Dr. Harriett S. Gainer, thank you for insisting that the tape of the Bible on healing be played continuously in my hospital room, and for being a strong and dedicated spiritual leader.

Thank you -Pastor Pearl Brown and Evangelist Mary Johnson for picking me up and driving me to church that Easter Sunday Morning.

Special thanks to: Brenda Whitaker - for being my personal angel during my hospital stay; Earl and Kathy McCall (former co-worker) - for your friendship and support during this dark period.

I would like to thank all of my family and friends who not only prayed for me but also gave support to my family.

Special thanks to Angela Hart for all that you do for the Hart family and to Bobbie Jean (Floyd) Jenkins for what you do for the Floyd family.

Thanks to Aunt Pricilla Hart, Evangelist Mildred Williams, Jennifer Williams, and Crystal Basley for listening and your spiritual encouragement; especially when I was at a stand-still in writing the book, you helped me focus on the direction I needed to take.

Thank you Dr. Judd Boasiotto, my professor in grad-school, for taking the extra time in your busy schedule to read over my testimony and for encouraging me to get it published. The testimony was rejected but hallelujah, it became a book.

Thank you Ulysses and Bernice Hart; Ulysses (Bubba) Hart Jr. and Pearl Hart- for letting me stay with each of you respectively until my wedding.

Special thanks to neighbor Willie Dowdell and my friend Cindy Lewis for helping me to understand what I needed to know about flowers, gardening, and yard work.

Thanks you Rev. Andrew Tilly (my childhood pastor in Pennsylvania) for giving me a scholarship to go to college, and to the Pleasant Hill Baptist church for my foundation.

I would like to thank Rev. Levy Breedlove and the Third Kiokee Baptist Church for embracing me as a member when I first came to Albany, and for training me on how to be a Girl Scout Leader.

I would like to thank family members and friends of the Second Bethesda Baptist Church and Pastor Rev. Rance Pettibone for being a part of my spiritual family and for your aide in my spiritual growth.

Thanks to Pastor, Bishop O. D. Burton, Sr. for your support, and the New Zion Hill Missionary Baptist Church for being a part of my spiritual family.

Thank you Reverend Ewing for marrying John and I. Thank you for your faithfulness, dedication to the Couple's Ministry, and for you and your wife Sue being friends to our family.

I want to thank my present pastor, Rev. Solomon Loud Jr. for being humble, anointed, and my father in the ministry. Thanks also to the New Beginning Missionary Baptist Church for your support and for being such a loving family.

Special thanks to: Douglas Stout; PB Studios for taking pictures for the book.

Special thanks to: Rev. Dr. Harriet S. Gainer for your dedication with editing this book.

Thanks to anyone who did something that I didn't know about or may have forgotten.

Last, but not least, I would like to thank my friend and colleague Laurie Anello. I met Laurie while I was attending a Jr. College in Pennsylvania; thirty-two years ago. You dropped a seed in my spirit eighteen years ago to write about my testimony. Thanks, Laurie, that seed will now grow and produce more fruit.

# About The Author

I guess I should begin by briefly telling you a little about me. Hopefully, you will feel that you are acquainted with me, and my testimony won't seem so intangible (unreachable) but will seem to be within reach. What God has done for me, He'll do for you. It is no secret what God can do.

I am originally from Johnstown, Pennsylvania. My parents had six children, four boys and two girls.I am the fifth child. After my oldest brother was born, my parents moved from Dawson, Georgia to Johnstown, Pennsylvania. During the summer, my sister- Belinda Hart- and I traveled by bus to the South. I met my husband in Albany, Georgia when I was a teenager. He lived two houses down the street from my aunt Bernice and uncle Ulysses Hart's house.

After I graduated from California State University in June of 1982, I stayed with my parents while I worked for a year with the Head Start Program as a home visitor. This enabled me to save my money so that I could fulfill a dream of returning to the "South." I stopped in Albany, Georgia first; where I planned to visit family members for a few days.

Needless to say, things didn't work out like I had planned. The day after I arrived in Albany, a friend of the family told John Floyd that I was in town. We've been together ever since that day. After visiting Florida, I returned to Pennsylvania to tell my mom and dad (Eva and Sammie Hart) that I was relocating to Albany, Georgia. I stayed with my uncle and aunt Ulysses and Bernice Hart for a year; then with Ulysses Jr. and Pearl Hart for half a year while John and I planned our wedding. We got married on February 16, 1985.

## Contact the Author

To purchase additional copies of this book for $12.00 plus $4.00 shipping and handling.

Email: alwdhf2010@gmail.com